LAW OF THE WILD

LAW OF
THE WILD

by

H. M. Peel

Dales Large Print Books
Long Preston, North Yorkshire,
BD23 4ND, England.

591.942

British Library Cataloguing in Publication Data.

Peel, H. M.
    Law of the wild.

        A catalogue record of this book is
        available from the British Library

        ISBN   978-1-84262-759-4 pbk

First published in Great Britain in 1975 by Rex Collings

Published in Large Print 2010 by arrangement with
H. M. Peel

Dales Large Print is an imprint of Library Magna Books Ltd.

Printed and bound in Great Britain by
T.J. (International) Ltd., Cornwall, PL28 8RW

Rededicated to

Ingeborg Schoppmann

FOREWORD BY
PROFESSOR DAVID BELLAMY

This is the true story about the wonder of an ordinary bit of countryside, set down for all to understand by the authoress who saw it happen before her very eyes. Like so many others she bought a cottage in the country and set about turning it, and its wild acre, into a home complete with ordered garden. One small corner she left in its semi-natural state, no weeding, no mowing, no chemicals, so it became her window onto another world. A vibrant world in which the law of the wild marked out the passing of the seasons with the awesomeness of existence. A never-ending, ever-changing drama of love and hate, happiness and fear, the joy of new life and the pain of death. The struggle for survival which has shaped the living world, of which we, like the keen observer who lets us eavesdrop on her story, are but a part. Uncared for, this tiny wilderness made her care enough to write this book.

Please read it with the care it deserves and then place it for ready reference beside a window in your house. Then if you are brave enough to see it all for yourself let part of your garden return to a semi-wild state so you may take good counsel from the seasons and find new hope in the law of the wild. Nature does not ask for much space but in return gives you a lifetime of understanding and hope for the future. Thank you for caring.

Signed DAVID BELLAMY. Bedburn 2000

CHAPTER ONE

The tree was old but strong. Its great girth, crinkled and scarred, rose high into the sky with branches sweeping out in an umbrella circle. The roots plunged deep down into red soil. Some channelling off to right and left, others, including the mighty tap root, bored a vertical line into the earth. Its solidity was majestic even when, as now, the naked branches were stark in the winter cold. The chestnut tree saw it all. It was shelter to animal and bird alike. A haven from the enemy, a covering against the storm, a peaceful spot from the summer sun's glare.

The grass under the sweep of the boughs was short, even stunted, but free from weeds. Three rotten chestnuts, ignored by the squirrel, lay buried beneath the snow. The remainder of the tree's nuts had been sound and swiftly cached for food.

There was a rabbit burrow to one side of the hedge, over which the tree towered and, at the other corner of the field's angle, was a fox's earth. Empty at the moment but suitable for habitation in the spring. In front of the tree the field was ploughed though hidden now under the frozen blanket. Behind, a small copse jumbled together solidly forming a black shadow when viewed from a distance.

It was the chestnut tree though which dominated all, no matter what the season or the mood of the weather. The small area was isolated and the top soil of poor quality. Cattle never roamed the field. The only human intrusion was the tractor and plough for the brief periods of sowing and reaping whatever the farmer thought would manage to thrive on such land.

In winter or summer, the animals and birds lived their lives under the shadow of the tree. And the tree knew it all. It observed in silence the matings and deaths; the insects and flowers, the life of the wild and the law that went with such wildlife.

It would moan in the wind and whisper its branches and leaves together on a summer's evening. It would stand silent, aloof and dignified as the birds greeted the dawn. It missed nothing. It knew all. It knew about the fox because the animal was an old friend of many years' knowledge and association and the tree understood its friend and felt its friend's suffering but it could not help. It could only watch and wait and offer the haven to be found in its branches or among its roots.

The fox halted in midstride with one paw raised. Nostrils twitched and lips curled back to show yellow fangs. The red-gold of his coat stood out vividly against the snow. From the hedge his progress had been slow and painstaking. Behind was a single line of tracks where, carefully and delicately, he had placed each hind pad down in the front one's mark.

The north wind veered unexpectedly. The cock pheasant caught the dangerous scent and with a chatter of wings lifted to safety. Baulked and disappointed, the old dog fox paused by the base of the tree. Slowly sinking back on his haunches, he considered the situation.

His belly griped savagely and saliva filled his mouth, anticipating the meat he had just missed. He had not eaten for two days now and hunger was making him desperate. The last meal had been two mice who, stupefied with the cold, had carelessly allowed themselves to be caught in the open.

He had to feed properly. Good, hot, red flesh or he too would go under to the savage

January weather.

The snow had not been too bad to start with. It was the severe frosts afterwards which had driven all game underground. For the meat eaters it had been a desperate time. The old fox had fared particularly badly. His reflexes had slowed with age. Twice he had missed a rabbit which, in his younger days, he would have grabbed after a few strides.

Once he had been beaten to it by the vixen. She was young and agile. She too had been hungry and without scruple. She had snapped the rabbit from under his very nose and made off at a gallop. He had turned half-heartedly after her then halted. She was a female. Her presence sacrosanct. That was the law of the wild.

He had tried the farmer's chicken coop again, knowing it to be a wasted trip. The guard wire was 2 feet higher and also plunged deep into the earth. He had regretted the trip. The sweet smell of all that feathered meat had had driven him into a short burst of frenzy. He had raced up and down outside the hen coop. He had wasted valuable time and energy, then more strength in a futile attempt to scale the wire. He was so hungry he had defied the farm dogs to prowl outside the house door. Hopefully he had looked for scraps but the rats had forestalled him.

He turned and walked back to the small copse of trees protected by the mighty chestnut. His home stamping ground. His eyes missed nothing. Anything which moved was edible. His brush drooped his feelings. His stomach churned angrily. It was eat or die.

Near to the chestnut's furthest root he halted, lifted his head and scented. Carefully he twitched, scanning his keen nostrils from left to right, up and down. A variety of scents came back to him which he quickly tabulated. The badger's sett a number of paces away which the fox ignored. He also ignored the birds overhead, too high. In a hole on his right, deep beyond reach, was a hibernating adder.

A robin cheeted at him from the top of a nearby hawthorn bush. The fox carefully eyed the bird. The number of strides necessary to reach the bush. The effort to make the leap before the bird could fly away, a quick experienced estimate told him no! There must be better game. He had to find more abundant meat and quickly.

He turned catching the scent full blast. Black lips drew back in a silent snarl. And ginger eyes flared like traffic lights from gold

15

to bright red. Ears flattened. With infinite caution he moved forward.

The scent was alluring. Saliva trickled down his jowls. He carefully tested each step, avoiding the ice which might crack. He reached the chestnut's trunk, sank to the ground and lay motionless – so still as to appear dead.

The fox knew his limitations where speed was concerned. But what he lacked in that direction he more than made up for in guile. He had the wild animal's supreme patience. Now that the hunt was on he stifled his agonising hunger pains. He concentrated.

Then movement showed through the copse's trees. Brown and red intermingled. A young fox trotted into the open, ten good leaps from the chestnut tree. A hare gripped firmly between his jaws.

The old fox's eyes flashed. That hare was going to be his. A young dog fox was fair game – unlike a vixen. A silent snarl rippled across his mask. Tensing his hind legs, twitching the tip of his brush, he calculated.

The youngster was blissfully unaware he had company. He had hunted well. He did not really want the hare and intended to cache it. His satisfied stomach blunted his instincts. He was too young to get away with such blatant behaviour.

He dropped the hare, sat down, licked his lips and, in a sudden burst of juvenile frivolity, boxed at the hare's body with his front paws.

The old fox exploded into action. He shot out from behind the chestnut tree. Yellow fangs bared. Jaws clicking in anticipation. Brush rigid as a pole.

The youngster had the shock of his life, but his sharper reflexes saved him. He leapt to one side, skidded on some ice, clutched with his claws and spun around. Ears back. White fangs ready for battle. He did not want the hare but neither was any other animal going to have it. That hare was *his* game.

The canny old dog fox ignored him. He dived for the hare. One quick snap of steel jaws and the sweet flesh was rigid between his teeth. He pivoted on his hocks, tendons straining, claws seeking a firm foothold, then sprang.

But the young one had recovered from his shock. He shot forward possessed with fury. His spring hurled his body into that of the older animal. He caught him fair and square and bowled him over. The hare flopped onto the snow.

With a flurry of pads the two foxes regained their feet and circled. The battlewise old fox eyed the terrain as well as his rival. He just sought an opportunity to grab the hare and bolt. Out and out fighting was not to his liking. He was too weak. This young, well-fed opponent would soon out-tire him – but he *must* have that meat.

Both animals threatened. Two sets of steel jaws clicked like sprung traps. Ears flat to their heads, nostrils flaring, they digested each other's scents.

The young fox sprang. He aimed a wild snap which, if it had connected, would have settled the issue there and then. The old dog fox rose on his hind legs, catching the blow on a thickly coated shoulder. He felt needle teeth drive through fur to sink in his skin. Unflinchingly, he took the blow then dropped. Limp and beaten. The younger animal fell for it. With a yowl of glee he straddled the prostrate body and aimed for the exposed neck.

The old dog fox rolled sideways. With perfect timing he knocked the other's legs flying. In a scurry of red fur and white snow the position was suddenly reversed. It was the old fox who snapped. His teeth were more accurate. They sank into fur, tissue and good, red blood.

The young fox howled in agony. Frantically he struggled to stand. The yellow teeth dug deeper with every second, seeking the pulsating jugular vein. The young fox panicked, straining to grab air, fighting to free the vice on his throat. Striking with his pads, his claws ripped chunks of red hair. Snow cascaded on both bodies.

The wise older fox stonily ignored the frantic struggling. He just increased his jaw-pressure. Refusing to be side-tracked by blows, undaunted as his body was flung around. His teeth sank deeper. They were very near now to the great vein.

In a paroxysm of terror the young fox gave one last heave. He scrambled erect, trembling violently. Blood cascaded down his coat. It stained the snow. He shuddered. Bracing himself he gave one gigantic leap into the air. Both animals still locked together landed back on the crisp snow with a heavy jar. The unexpected jolt broke the lethal grip. The yellow teeth slipped and parted.

The young fox lurched to the left. He forced his legs to hurry, knowing his strength was draining away. He shook his muzzle. Blood sprayed through the air. The old dog tensed for a final spring. He knew victory – and the hare – were his.

As if from nowhere, in that split second, the crafty vixen shot between them both. With one graceful swoop she grabbed the hare and turned to flee. The old fox yowled in rage. He turned to this new intruder. The younger fox grabbed the chance and fled a jerky retreat.

The vixen, playing upon her sex, snarled warningly at the dog. For two seconds the starving fox hesitated. To attack a future mate was against the law of the wild. Instinct struggled against starvation. The vixen watched alertly, hare gripped firmly between her teeth. She knew full well the emotions tearing at the old fox.

In a way she was interested in him. The hare tasted good in her mouth yet she too was being moved by instinct. This was the time of the year when the solitary roaming foxes started seeking out their mates. Battle had already been done. Not over her but over the second most important thing in life – meat. Her snarls quietened.

The old dog had regained his wind while he stared at the vixen. The tantalising aroma of the meat decided him. He sprang – the law forgotten. The vixen dropped the hare and shot to the left, knowing this was not the time to argue.

The fox caught the hare's body, dropped to his haunches and started tearing at the meat. Eating ravenously, he still kept a wary eye on the vixen. He bolted the kill, gobbling savagely. At long last he felt the gripes go from his belly. It had been a large buck hare, enough even to satisfy the fox's voracious appetite. Stuffed to bursting he lay down licking his lips. He was at peace with the world. Fresh life burst inside his body.

The vixen eyed him doubtfully. She plucked up courage and approached. She grabbed what was left of the carcase. With a benevolent eye the dog watched her. Feelings coursed through him. Suddenly he was aware that spring was only around the corner.

He stood and carefully approached the vixen, whining to her. Her bottom lip curled back but her snarl slowly changed to a throaty growl, soft without menace.

Encouraged, the dog lowered his mask and touched muzzles then backed, turning invitingly. Making up her mind she padded after him, breaking into a lope. Running shoulder to shoulder, the two foxes slipped through the hedge. From now on they were mates. They would hunt, breed and stay together until the cubs-to-be were themselves adult.

The tree had silently watched the battle. One of so many which had taken place during its life. It was glad of the outcome. The old dog was a friend of many years' standing. As the two ran off together the tree understood. They would be back sometime. Once the snow and frost had gone the vixen would come to the earth. When her time was near and she wanted a safe haven for her cubs, she would find the earth. The old fox himself had been born there many years ago. He would show her, then respectfully retreat from an affair which did not concern him.

The tree was sad for the beaten animal but it was, after all, the simple law of the wild. There was only ever one victor. The wild had no place for the weak or foolish and during vicious weather conditions only the best of any species was allowed to live to perpetuate its kind.

The young fox had been found lacking in cunning. He had to pay. It had been his first winter, his first lethal fight – and his very own sire had defeated him. Without whimper or groan the young fox accepted the law. He had lost. With the silent stoicism of the wild he lay down in the undergrowth of the copse and quietly died.

The tree's furthermost branch reached

out and hovered over the body; a naked, frost-covered branch with the sap still as the tree waited for spring's life to burst inside and frozen buds to become beautiful. Win or die. Eat or be eaten. And in its rightful turn the dead fox would save other lives. Nothing was wasted in the wild. Everything had a time and place and a purpose.

It was a harsh time too for the rabbits. Many of them had died. The ground was covered with a six inch blanket of frozen snow with a crisp top covering which defied their tiny claws.

Fifty yards from the tree's furthermost root a small colony of rabbits had hopefully established themselves the previous summer. They had found one ancient burrow and rapidly developed a small town with their tunnels running under the hedge and opening into the field and the copse.

It was a suitable place for a rabbit colony. They had the best of both the field and trees. When too hot they could retreat underground or shelter under the chestnut tree. The food in the summer and autumn had been abundant. The hedgerows were rich with plant life. The copse, where saplings and shrubs fought for sun and life, was another excellent plant larder.

Of course, there was a dangerous fox earth near the giant tree but, when food was plentiful, the rabbits had been left in peace. They knew full well that few foxes would kill their neighbours. They preferred to keep that meat supply for emergencies only. It was a sensible law. Known to both rabbit and fox and equally understood.

The unusual length and severity of the winter though had made the rabbits' lives precarious. The vixen had left the earth when her cubs became independent but though vacant now the rabbits knew, only too well, that any fox thought nothing of covering miles when his belly griped for food and his mood was savage.

But they too had to eat to live. They were warm underground, oblivious to the cold above their warren. Above though life was deadly. The grass had long been hidden under frozen snow which defied their claws. The undergrowth which abounded the hedges was white, stiff and held little nutriment to satisfy their hunger.

In the copse the cold had dissipated a little and they had been able to gnaw the bark from smaller saplings and chew some plants.

Such forays were hazardous. There were

more than the fox on the prowl. The relentless weasel was dreaded even more than the fox.

The large buck rabbit, king of the warren, battle-scarred from a long and lucky life, and an inveterate bully, saved them often. His uncanny hearing plus the sensitivity of his feet alerted them. The rapid drum-drumming of danger was never questioned by the colony. The buck rabbit's hind feet, used for fighting as well as drumming, was always followed by the white scut of his tail flashing a visual danger as he led the stampede back to the safety of the warren.

Guaranteed safety against a fox but not foolproof when the slimline weasel was hungry.

Because of his prowess as a fighter and scout the buck rabbit had the first and best food. The does and young gave way respectfully to him. The young bucks also learned to do this if they wished to avoid sudden punishment. The tough buck reigned supreme in his kingdom and would continue to do so until such time as an up-and-coming buck out-fought him. The prize for such a victory was, as always, the right to mate the female of the species and so produce the strongest young.

The animals' first and most respected law.

The buck rabbit was not averse to some of his young starving too. It was only right that the weak should die. It was important though that he always ate. To guard and fight he had to have strength and speed.

The constant journeys for food stretched the buck rabbit's nerves to breaking point and his temper, never peaceful, was constantly boiled with anxiety.

The climax had to come. The tree had seen it happen so many times before during its long life.

The buck rabbit was hungry as usual. There had been another sharp night frost and when dawn did come and the rabbits cautiously emerged from their warren, the buck's temper had been at a snappy point.

He had bowled over a doe impatiently, thumped a last season's buck with his powerful hind legs for no reason at all, then bounded impetuously through the icy ditch into the copse.

The weasel was equally hungry. The difference between the two animals was the unmatched ferocity and fearlessness of the weasel – coupled with a higher degree of intelligence – and the buck's lack of foresight.

It was only when too late did the buck catch the weasel's acrid scent. He jumped high, landed with drumming feet and fled. The weasel shot after him. Thin, elegantly tapered in length and with eyes of fire, the weasel followed.

The rabbits had vanished at the first warning boom from the buck's feet. The buck rabbit, in utter panic, threw himself through the ditch and bounded across the field. The weasel glided after him.

The rabbit knew he was doomed. No weasel had ever learned to give up once on the trail of meat. Even the fox stepped aside when weasels hunted in a pack. The rabbit skidded over the hard-packed snow and tried every trick he knew as the weasel closed. He jumped, turned in mid-air and thudded out with his feet. The weasel was too low-slung and the blow missed. So the rabbit bolted and created a safe gap, then was forced to stop for breath. The weasel slunk up again and now the buck rabbit froze.

He could not help but stare back at the fire of the two small eyes. Death was inches away and he was utterly hypnotized. He slumped helplessly and waited to die. He had been careless. Now he must pay. *That* was the law.

The tree saw it all and understood. Everything must eat something to survive itself. Only the largest animal, the fox, had no direct enemy to eat it.

The chestnut tree understood so well because it too, in its younger days, had been forced to fight and hope for luck. A handful of loose nuts, collected and then forgotten by a squirrel, had thrust out roots one spring. The nut which had the largest root obtained the best soil and took the most nourishment.

The red conker, large to start with, had been lucky enough to have a head start. It had soon crowded out its rivals, thrust down a root, sucked up the precious food from the soil and, by the first winter, was a daring shoot poking through the soil.

Those first months were lucky ones. *That* winter had been mild and green. There had been enough vegetation for the herbivorous animals without them having to nibble the shoot's dainty top. Then another stroke of luck had helped the baby tree. A wind had uprooted a scraggy hawthorn bush and blown it over the chestnut. The bush dried, the sharp twigs acted as barbed wire and the wild animals never bothered to push through the prickles for the chestnut's shoot.

By the time those prickles had rotted the nut was a small sapling standing three feet high. A sharp winter came and the young tree nearly died. Its attacker was another rabbit. This rabbit had been as hungry as any grass eater when frost strikes. The young sapling had seemed a wonderful meal. The rabbit, a wandering doe, had stood on her hind legs and started stripping the sweet-tasting bark from the sapling in long, thin strips.

The tree had known it was doomed now. Without its protective bark it would die instantly. The doe nibbled happily on, starting to work around in a circle. Once complete the circle would spell the chestnut's doom as certainly as any woodsman's axe.

It was a fox though who unwittingly saved the day. A feeding rabbit, with careless defences, was a target not to be missed. It had taken only one snap from white-toothed jaws to provide the fox with the meal and save the sapling's life.

It had been tough for the young tree, touch and go. A sudden change in the weather, an unexpected burst of spring sun had made the sap rise. It had churned slowly up the dainty trunk and along the slender strip of bark left intact. The outcome had been in the balance for many days then, very slowly, the huge wound had started to heal over and the tree began to live properly again.

There had been a scar which, as the tree grew, had stretched until now, high up the massive trunk it was almost invisible where the wind, weather and moss had shaded it.

The tree knew though that those had been its most dangerous days. Now its immense strength and size were protection alone. In its sheer majesty nothing could hurt it – except perhaps some minute creature like a wood boring insect almost too small for any to see.

Such was the relentless circle. The law of the wild.

The tree saw the two foxes often during the weeks which followed. They roamed far and wide but regularly returned to the area around the chestnut and spent their court-ship time playfully fighting.

The dog fox allowed the vixen her way, pandering to her whims. He could afford to now. With the sharper speed from his mate he did not go hungry so often, as this, coupled with his considerable cunning, kept them reasonably well supplied with food.

The vixen had already discovered the earth but she was not yet ready to house-hunt seriously. It was more fun to hunt with her mate, to roam, seek, then stalk for their meat.

With food in their bellies the foxes had energy to play. The frozen snow was pleasant now. They rolled in it, taking it in turns to straddle each other, growling, threatening with their teeth and even snapping in mock anger.

While they played all other creatures stayed silent and hidden. Even with full bellies two foxes in mid-winter were not to be trifled with, but the play time of the foxes meant unnecessary hunger for others. No rabbit dare wander for food. Only the birds were unconcerned.

The boldest was the male robin who had staked his patch with care. The chestnut tree was the centre of his patch while his territory extended over some of the field and half of the copse.

The robin was violently jealous of his territory and aggressive enough to ward off any other bird even though it was nowhere near nesting time. The bird's black eyes were very bright, contrasting vividly with the red breast as the robin perched openly on the tree's branches in the still air, but selected a more sheltered hedge when the wind gusted.

The cock robin had his eye on a dainty female but his advances had been few and uncertain. He needed the nudge of spring sunshine to press his case and show what a splendid fellow he was.

The tree understood the bird. It also knew the pattern of the courtship to come and even anticipated the house-building which was bound to take place in the hedge to the right.

It fully understood the robin's present behaviour. Food was very scarce and the small bird was hard pressed at times to keep alive. During the very coldest of the weather the robin had sat mournfully in the hedge, his feathers fluffed out to keep in the in-sulating air warmed against his fragile body.

The robin kept up a bold front though. He would twitter and sing daring the wild to defy him but his temper was unpredictable. When angered his body seemed to swell and any bird foolish enough to perch on his tree, the very hub of his patch, was immediately dealt with. If the same size – and even a little larger – the robin would hurl himself into violent war. Pecking, screaming outrage and driving off the unfortunate traveller with a barrage of abuse. Even the larger birds fared little better. The robin had sense enough not to waste his frail strength against wandering rooks and seagulls but he made his feelings perfectly plain.

This was *his* patch. He would fight to the death to keep it.

They were all part and parcel of the wild's gigantic plan. Everything had a place and there was a place for everything but only when the wild's immutable laws were observed.

Each species must mate only with its own kind. The law frowned on hybrids and mutations. Every single animal, bird and insect would respond only to the agreed courtship of his particular kind. Sparrow would not mate with robin. Fox thus disdained badger. Chestnut tree would only produce nuts when pollinated from chestnut flowers.

None of which had been taught to any young but were handed down in the form of inborn instinct, pure and undiluted through the passage of time.

CHAPTER TWO

The first positive signs of spring came in the middle of February. The wind at last changed from the north to the east and, though still anything but warm, the snow began to recede. A weak sun appeared for a few hours in the middle of some days and, on others, a driving rain lashed the tree.

The snow reluctantly gave up its grip on the earth and grudgingly allowed grass to appear again. Not fresh grass but dirty stuff, the blades bent and split where snow and frost had crushed and frozen.

But the grass was resilient, almost impossible to kill. Even the feeble sun had an effect. It straightened out the blades and with the rain's help washed away the grime left from the snow.

Down by the hedge, just at the top of the ditch, the first flower tentatively showed. During the frozen weeks it had been kept warm by the snow's blanket and, ever eager to be the first flower of the year, the snowdrops drooped their white bells under the sun and swayed daintily in the wind.

The tree was not quite ready for fresh life. It would take more than this feeble sun to make its sap rise but it would be ready. Dormant buds were on its branches and twigs. Now they had been washed with the rain the tree smelled good, wholesome and sweet.

The earth at the base of the trunk was soggy and criss-crossed with animals' trails as they moved about more easily in their perpetual quest for food.

For some weeks the foxes had not appeared and the tree wondered uneasily if anything had happened. Had the old dog fox met his match at last in a fight? Was the vixen now mate to another?

But the two foxes appeared suddenly just as the dawn broke. The old dog in the lead, the vixen warily at his rear, suspiciously scenting the air. The dog fox was confident, sure of himself and familiar with the territory. The tree was an old friend, the oldest friend he had.

This has been where he had spent his early days as a cub. It was here he had been reared and it was nearly always to this favourite spot that he brought his current mate. There were other more practical reasons too.

The land's lie suited him. There was cover in the copse. A good view over the open field. Shelter against bad weather and shade under a hot sun. During the good months of fine weather game abounded in the trees and hedges. Water was always available in the copse where a tiny spring seeped to the surface to trickle westwards in a narrow stream. It was good, sweet water. All the animals used it and it made the fox's hunting so much easier if hard pressed to feed his family.

Not all of his mates had approved the area but he was a cunning old fox. He knew better than to use force. The earth was years old, well used and a most desirable fox residence. If a vixen disdained the earth, if she was so foolish that she could not recognize a good thing when viewed then the dog would lie, play and coax her into following his plans.

The vixen sat and surveyed the area. She had spotted the earth as soon as they had pushed through the hedge and now she held a private debate with herself.

She could see from where she sat that the earth's entrance was wide and also protected by the tree. She cocked her head to one side, regarded the dog fox lying down, panting slightly, then stood and slowly walked forward to inspect.

The vixen sniffed at the earth's entrance. It had a homely foxy smell which told her of many past occupations. She crinkled her sensitive nostrils, inhaling deeply and padded forward.

The earth sloped slightly downhill for about ten feet then branched sharply to the right where it widened into the actual den. It was dry and wide enough for a vixen and her cubs to live in comfort. Where the branch occurred there was another small junction enabling any fox to turn quickly and attack a pursuer.

The vixen took her time investigating the proffered home. She sniffed all round, scratched the hard packed earth, turned in the junction and lay down, head on her front paws.

She knew her mate was waiting patiently outside. She was in no hurry to join him. This was her realm. This was her time, her cubs would be born in a few weeks' time. Out of all the earths she had visited this was the most superior. She had no work to do to make it habitable, which suited her. Like all of her breed, the vixen was a lazy and indifferent housekeeper. She would only dig her own earth as a last desperate measure.

Finally, she was satisfied with her inspection. She padded back to her mate. The older fox stood and watched her approach. His brush wagged hopefully. They touched muzzles and she showed her agreement and, in pleasure at her acceptance, the dog fox pranced a few paces like a new season's cub, then trotted off. The vixen followed. She was hungry again. A mouthful or two would be agreeable to her right now, then she would move into her new home while the old fox slept out near the ditch. On guard nearby but definitely away from the earth itself.

It was only when really dark did the badger like to leave his sett and that night he left in a very bad temper. He had only moved into this particular home the previous autumn. Although he knew of the presence of the foxes' earth it had not then been occupied. The previous season's cubs had become adult and were making their own way in life.

The badger had known many setts but never one quite as good as this near the chestnut tree. It had originally been a small rabbit burrow but the badger had spent many hours and much labour in altering it to suit his fastidious taste.

He was a perfectionist and one armed with splendid tools to make a perfect home. The claws, especially those on his front paws, were long and powerful. Where digging was concerned the badger was unsurpassed in the animal world.

He had laboured to widen the tunnel to suit himself, then had carefully removed every particle of soil and litter. He took it away and hid it. Then he scrupulously cleaned his sett until it was sweet-smelling and to his liking. Like all badgers he was fastidious about cleanliness. He never fouled the land near his home but always walked a distance away and, like a cat, covered his droppings with soil.

When he came out into the dark, raw night he was appalled at the stench which came from the earth as he passed. He knew instantly the vixen was inside and her mate would be watching from nearby. Immediately his temper flared. The filth, the indescribable stink in an area adjacent to his carefully built home, was almost too much. His lips curled back and he rumbled to himself in disgust as he stopped.

The moon peeped from behind a cloud

and glowed down on him. His long snout, with the broad white stripe running from between the ears to his damp nose, glistened as he flickered his ears. Although basically a very shy animal the badger, just then, was in the frame of mind which would brook no argument from any animal.

The tree knew that in an out and out death fight the fox should win; it also knew the badger's powerful claws could inflict barbarous wounds. It was uneasy. It now had two friends who had taken up home under its shelter but two neighbours who were certainly not meant to live together amicably because of their differing standards of housekeeping.

The badger was reluctant to move. His mate would also soon bear young. It would require tremendous effort to find and make another set ready at such short notice. The foxes were obviously settled in their home.

The only slight gleam of hope was that earth and sett were apart from each other by a distance of twenty yards. Providing the wind did not blow from earth to sett all might be well. The tree knew that no self-respecting badger would long tolerate the stench and dirty habits of any vixen.

The tree also knew that where diet was

concerned the two animals would rarely clash. The badger lived mainly on roots, fruit, snails, honey and sometimes young rabbits as well as wasps and bees. With his loose, almost hanging skin, he was impervious to stings.

Although the fox had an equally voracious appetite, he preferred flesh. If the weather were kind while both animals were rearing their respective young and food was, consequently, abundant, they would not clash.

It was the old, old story of a clean neighbour having to tolerate a dirty one. Fortunately, the wind, as often as not, blew from the west, which meant the scents in the air would travel from the badger's sett to the foxes' earth. If the position had been reversed the badger might have been compelled to seek a home elsewhere.

The tree knew what the badger's frame of mind would then be if it accidentally met the fox. Like all other members of the weasel family the badger, although basically such a peaceful animal, could be the worst antagonist of all when provoked beyond endurance.

Grumbling to himself the badger shuffled off down the track. He rolled with his odd gait, not unlike a young pig.

The dog fox watched him disappear. His

ears twitched as he lay frozen and silent. The only movements were from the rapid shifting of his bright eyes when the moon shone. Once, many years ago, when a very green fox, he had tangled with a badger. He had come off worse and been left with a scar down one shoulder which, even now, was faintly visible where the hair ran a shade darker. Since then, the fox had always respected the badger's claws and, more to the point, his great fighting ability.

If he had met the badger in the winter months when starving, the old fox would have attacked without hesitation. Now, with a full belly, a warm bed in the hedge and his mate sleeping in safety he was more than happy to let his neighbour pass unchecked.

The rabbits though were distinctly unhappy but quite powerless to alter the situation. They now had another buck in charge of their warren. He was not battle-wise and only kept his place as leader of the community because he was the largest rabbit and no other buck had yet thought of a way to defeat him in battle.

The does were uneasy about the foxes. Once spring came properly and food abounded their situation would ease. As it was, two adult foxes could consume a lot of rabbits if inclined and, though there was the law not to kill game on the doorstep but to leave it for emergencies, the warren was in a constant state of dither.

The tree knew the warren would settle down in time. Their young would soon appear on the scene. They would have other far more important matters to occupy them. Already there were signs they were burrowing again; busy making their backdoors for emergency escapes if the warren were invaded by enemies like a pack of savage weasels.

One of the emergency tunnels came up under the far hedge near to a thick clump of couch grass. It was indiscernible to the eye and, because it was for emergency only and not used regularly, no tracks lead away from it. The tree doubted whether even the wily dog fox knew of its existence yet.

During that month there was one particularly warm day when the sun shone for five whole hours bathing the tree in beauty and heat before the cool evening wind rose again.

The squirrel woke up. He had enjoyed another short sleep and was hungry now. Like all of his kind he had wisely gathered a choice store of nuts during the autumn. Halfway up the trunk of the mighty tree was the hole where, many years ago, a branch had been shorn with lightning. The hole was about a foot deep and made a perfect winter home for the squirrel. He did have his drey, his nest which he shared with his mate. A nest the two of them had used for more than one season. This was high, almost at the top of the tree and was made from twigs, moss, leaves and grass. The squirrel knew the nest was still there; it had been well built in the first place and could withstand most of the winter storms. There might be some patching to do, perhaps even a little decorating but the nest would not require much work before the young arrived.

The first consideration was food. With small eyes twinkling in the sun the squirrel ran half-way down the trunk, paused to survey all was well with no obvious danger, then he raced the rest of the distance jumping the last few feet. His thick tail bushed out like a parachute and made his landing feather-light.

With quick movements the squirrel hurried through the hedge to the base of a blackthorn tree. Unerringly he started to dig with his tiny paws. Five inches down he found his treasured nuts, hidden with so much loving care so many months ago.

He picked up a nut, held it neatly between his paws and chewed quickly. His empty stomach demanded immediate and total fulfillment. The once shining nut, now dark and dank, was swiftly consumed to be followed by more.

By now, the squirrel was slowing down. As his stomach filled he became aware that it was not quite as warm as he had first thought. The air was thin and cold to him. His little dark hole appeared very inviting. The tree was so near but there was one more nut. Then this little larder would be finished.

The squirrel bent for the nut. The wind changed a point to the east and saved the squirrel's life. The sharp, acrid tang of fox flashed across his nostrils. Without thought or glance the squirrel shot forward, the nut dropping from his paws. He raced across to his tree, his gait a mixture of run and bound, while his thick tail waved like a banner.

The vixen bounded eagerly after him but she knew she had no real chance. She was slower now, the cubs lying heavy in her abdomen. The dog fox might have succeeded.

The squirrel leaped two feet high and grasped the solid trunk and moved upwards.

His progress was swift and sure. His feet grasped the rigid bark while his tail gave him balance. Only when he knew he was safe did he dare to pause and look back.

The vixen sat and returned his stare. Her jaws open, tongue lolling at the meal just missed. Bold and defiant now, the squirrel swore down at her then, honour satisfied, he climbed high to his dear little hole.

The cock robin had watched the drama below. He was totally unconcerned as he had far more important matters to deal with now. His nest site had been selected with care and prudence. It was high and also deeply hidden in the very centre of the hedge yet, at the same time, it would enable the robin to fly easily to his tree. His throne. The very centre of his realm.

A female was showing him a little attention though not, as yet, giving to the cock bird all the attention and adulation that he considered his masculine status warranted. But that did not matter just yet.

Let a little more spring weather appear and the robin's courtship would become arduous and sincere. No female could possibly fail to respond. In the meantime, as he sat on his slender twig, the robin studied his nest site, approved his wisdom and congratulated himself with a burst of merry song.

The tree itself was slowly, very slowly, getting ready to stir into new life. Deep below the ground, far lower than animal or insect could travel, the roots slowly throbbed with the anticipation of spring. Each massive root ended in a thin, tapering point with sensitive hairs which provided the food and water for the life of the giant so far above. A tremendous surge of nourishment would soon be needed to succour the buds, leaves and flowers to come.

The earth was generous. The top soil was rich with humus. Below was a layer of clay and under that compressed vegetation which, in thousands of years, might perhaps turn into coal.

In the rich soil lived some of the tree's best friends. Without them, the great roots would have had to travel far for food. The earthworms gathered in great numbers attracted by the soil itself which they in turn enriched even more with their constant travels, burrows and eating.

They patiently swallowed all the vegetable matter they met, depositing their waste after them. They made thousands of minute burrows and at the mouths of these they would slowly draw down into the soil tiny particles of vegetation for future consumption.

Their constant activity turned the soil over. Their ceaseless tunnelling brought goodness from the surface deep down into the blackness of the earth and the tree thrived as the roots devoured the offerings left by the worms.

The tree was also host to another insect. One with a highly developed instinct and even a certain degree of memory. The ants had a fairly large colony at the base of the tree. They were still dormant. The weather had to be warmer than it was but the tree knew that, once stirred into life, its base would hum with constant activity.

Their nest was thrust deep into the ground where the earth was crumbly and lent itself to easy tunnelling between two great roots. The land itself sloped away from the tree and water never collected. A flood was impossible. The passages and chambers went into the ground a distance of twelve inches and were hidden from view by a small collection of dead leaves, twigs and nut cases which had formed into a solid, stiff mass over the undisturbed years.

There was some danger to the ants now that the badger had taken up residence nearby but there was danger, to some degree or other, for any creature living wild. With their ability to multiply so well the tree knew there was little fear these faithful friends would disappear entirely.

The great chestnut tree, the pinnacle of the area, was the centre of wildlife itself. The very apex to the creatures whether they lived above, on, or below the soil level. Without the great tree many would not be there. And as the tree lived, so did they. The tree not only provided shade and shelter but it was also the most prominent landmark for miles around. A multitude of game trails crossed and recrossed all within feet of tree's base. The mighty top boughs were a well-known resting place for migratory birds and often, during the late autumn, the tree would be smothered with black, white and brown bodies as birds jostled themselves into a comfortable position for a night's rest before heading into all points of the compass.

No load was ever too much for the tree but no wild friend could stay with it for ever. They went their ways. They died. Only the tree lived on and on. It made fresh friends. Its boughs gave sympathetic haven to all while it spread a rich, green carpet at its base which was soft for the animals' feet. It sprinkled tear drops of dew at dawn giving coolness which soothed. Above all it gave peace and quiet which all those of the wild needed.

It was always there. The magnificent tree, still, dark and silent; home to so many and shelter to all. Foe to none. And always alone. That too was also the law.

CHAPTER THREE

Winter was reluctant to retreat. It threw a white mailed fist down on the earth in one final gesture. Spring fought back and pushed a sunny invasion inexorably forward, day by relentless day.

The frost appeared each dusk, gripped the land in a hard embrace until by dawn everything lay under a thick layer of white crystals. The sky was cloudless, the air still and sharp. The first ray of the sun was no more than a tentative yellow gesture but, as the hours passed, and the sun shifted a little higher in the sky, the white hoar frost would melt and slither away to be replaced by the fresh dampness of March.

Infinitely slowly, the sun became stronger and the air warmer. It was a fierce environmental struggle which lasted nearly two weeks before winter finally capitulated to the west wind and rain.

To the wild creatures it was a time to stand still and wait just a little longer before the burst of breeding activity commenced.

Anyone who ignored winter's final ferocious gesture would pay with their lives. That was the law.

The creatures knew this only too well. They watched stoically and waited patiently. One did not. It was bold, foolhardy and defied the law. It had to pay for such stupidity with death. Excuses were never accepted.

That particular mid-day was mild to the point of being warm. No trace of the previous night's frost appeared to remain. Only the rock-hard earth in the constant shadow of the hedge was a reminder of the ice-cold nights still to come.

It was a first season's bee. A young worker. Inexperienced, recently hatched and chosen as a scout to see what flowers were available which might yield some pollen for honey and how far these were from the hive.

The sun bedazzled the bee. Such a glorious yellow! Such warmth upon its tiny back and fragile wings. It flew recklessly far from the hive, drugged with the power of flight and the sun on its back. The heady freedom of space. The snowdrops – such a wealth of early sweetness!

It came to rest on one of the tree's twigs. A dot of an insect which paused for a moment in time. The tree knew better because it was late afternoon. The sun was low on the horizon and in minutes it would vanish. Once that happened the bee was doomed. That dainty – but delicate – body must have warmth and sun. The bee, above all other life, could not survive in cold, sterile air. Once the sun vanished the air temperature would change in less than a minute.

The bee realised this danger too late. Its flower drugged brain cleared. Impulses went down to the wings and they struggled valiantly to make the flight. Already though, the air had cooled and the wings were affected. They moved feverishly then gradually slowed. As the bee became colder the impulses stilled. It crouched on the twig, made one final, frantic effort to obtain flight then slumped down exhausted with effort and temperature's drastic change. Its head stilled, its body stiffened and its little legs slowly buckled at the joints.

Only balance kept it on the twig. The tree waited. The bee died quickly, numbed with cold and, with balance gone, the small body fluttered from the twig and drifted down to the earth by the great trunk. It fell between two of last autumn's brown leaves and vanished from sight. The law had again exacted due payment from those who defied her basic rules.

The tree was not so foolhardy. The thousands of buds on the tree were firm and hard and though the sap was starting to move the buds would not advance their progress until winter finally vanished and all was safe.

This was finally assured when, one dawn, a gentle breeze fluffed through the air from the west. For the first time in weeks the sky was dappled with puff-balls of grey clouds which slowly thickened and deepened as the wind increased in strength.

The first rain was little more than a mist which gradually strengthened into separate droplets of soft water. This turned into a real rain, steady, clean and welcome. The wind slanted the rain at an angle and increased its pressure until the drops stung the tree's bark and danced upon the earth to seek out, penetrate and destroy the last vestiges of winter's frosts.

As the weather changed so did the vixen's temper. She was heavy and cumbersome, slow-moving and fretful. It was the dog fox who hunted for both of them now. He had little trouble finding enough meat and did not have to range far for his hunting. The copse alone provided many voles and birds.

Occasionally he would roam further afield to bring his mate back a juicy rabbit. The neighbouring warren he studiously ignored. That was their emergency meat supply.

Like nearly all of her kind the vixen's normal temperament was a combination of impish mischief and downright curiosity. As the time for the cubs' birth neared she became snappish and quarrelsome.

The dog fox, many times a sire and wise to the ways of vixens at this time of the year, only ever approached his mate with prudence and caution. He kept well away from the mouth of the earth. That was the vixen's domain now and, so irritable had she become, the dog fox made sure he gave no cause for offence by inadvertent trespassing. The vixen's teeth were sharp and her jaws quick. Her courage never in doubt at any time – let alone when she was near producing a litter of cubs.

On the day it finally stopped raining the vixen, with her mate near her side, stood by the tree's trunk. The dog fox was eager to go for a hunt. He trotted a few paces then halted, turned and waited for the vixen to follow.

She stood uncertainly and ignored his pleading eyes and lolling tongue. Instinct prodded at her. She eyed her earth then with slow steps turned and headed towards the dark entrance. Without hesitation or backward glance she stepped into the welcome darkness and padded down to the fork then turned into the chamber. She scratched the earth with one paw, turned round twice then slowly lay down. Her muzzle pointed towards the exit. Her thick brush draped neatly over her paws. She rested and waited. She was on her own and she welcomed none. Soon, very soon, she would be racked with pain but no sound would issue from her jaws. That which would happen to her was only another natural law which she would accept willingly because after the pain would come the exquisite pleasure of enjoying her cubs.

The dog fox understood. This had happened to him so many times before. He did not exist for the time being but he would be of immense value later. He too must wait. He must feed himself and lie in his makeshift den in the hedge. His job was to be vigilant, patient and ready when needed. He must not, under any circumstances, approach – let alone set paw in – that now sacrosanct earth.

He trotted through the copse, bolted some field mice, filled his stomach and returned to the hedge. He lay muzzle on black tipped brush. His ears pricked for the smallest sound, his eyes half shut but his nerves and senses at the alert. He waited with the incredible patience and understanding of the wild animal.

The tree waited with him. Aloof, silent and dignified with the majesty of many years, the great chestnut spread its branches over the fox's hiding place. With the warmer weather the tree had been stirred into its own activity. The roots had probed for extra nourishment. The sap had climbed. The countless buds were now swollen and sticky, poised ready to burst into tender leaves. The tree understood both foxes so well because it too was on the verge of undergoing its own peculiar form of birth and new life.

The dog fox waited two nights. He left his vigil only to snatch food before resuming his guard station. No sound reached him from the earth and he did not expect any. The other creatures of the wild passed his lair as they went about the activities of their old lives. The fox ignored them all. His ears might twitch and identify the passing parade but his eyes never wandered from the earth.

His patience was finally rewarded. He heard a minute sound and stood with his ears pointed forward. His head was tilted to one side to obtain better vision. His brush was horizontal, the only movement being a nervous twitching from the tip.

The vixen's head appeared at the earth's mouth. She looked around, saw her mate then stepped slowly out into the open. She was gaunt and bedraggled. Her body had changed shape. Her ribs stood out. She was hungry and thirsty.

The dog fox stood and greeted her with a gentle touch of muzzles. His whole body quivered with barely suppressed excitement. The vixen lowered her head and sucked greedily at the water in the ditch. It took a long time to satisfy her thirst but, finally, she stopped. The water dripped down from her whiskers as she looked pointedly at her mate. No sound passed between them before the vixen turned and made her way back into the earth again.

Inside the chamber she lay down carefully, her four cubs clambered feebly over her and demanded milk, sleep and attention at the same time. She acquiesced to their demands while she listened intently. She was being torn in two. The cubs' demands were hers to satisfy with immediate attention but her belly was empty. Without meat and the strength given by food her cubs would only suffer.

The vixen's ears were alert. She heard the tiny sound, interpreted it and stood. The cubs tumbled from her crying their protest at such harsh treatment. The vixen went to the entrance and saliva filled her jaws. The rabbit was freshly killed. It was manna from heaven. She fell upon the sweet meat and savaged the flesh wildly. Her powerful teeth flashed white and sharp as they severed the meat into neat portions. She ate quickly and well.

Fresh strength pulsed through her veins. Good milk would now flow in her body in plenty. Her mate was doing his job. She must do hers and rear the cubs to strength and safe adulthood.

The robin conquered! He won his mate but only after a furious battle. A fight the like of which the tree had not seen for many a long year.

The small bird had to call upon all his strength and fury because the rival robin also liked the area around the tree. Further he had decided that the ditch's bank would make a far superior nest for *his* chosen mate than the local robin's proposed housing site in the hawthorn hedge.

The local robin could hardly believe his beady, black eyes when a hostile robin flew around *his* territory then up into the chestnut tree, perched on a slender branch and burst into a song which any self-respecting robin knew was nothing but a verbal declaration of war.

The two cock birds started with a skirmishing war. They flew at each other, banked suddenly to one side, hurled strong language, and generally eyed up their respective strengths. They were equally matched in size and age. They both had hen birds to watch and praise their performances and, also, to snub any loser. They had all to gain by victory and everything to lose in defeat.

The local robin had a slight edge in that the territory around the chestnut tree was his from long ownership. His rival was an interloper who was trying to obtain squatter's rights.

There could only be one ending and the tree resigned itself to the inevitable fight. The two birds, driven to an uncontrollable pitch of masculine fury, threw themselves together in midair. Their wings beat wildly as two beaks stabbed with ferocity. Both birds were quick but, even then, feathers started to fly downwards.

The local robin was goaded by desperation into a frenzy of activity which, the tree knew, could not be sustained for very long. The small – but sharp – beak stabbed and pecked while two wings buffeted as the birds landed on the grass and resumed their fight with little foot-high jumps in the air.

The rival robin was taken aback. He wanted to nest in the bank. He was prepared to fight for this honour. He was not prepared to commit suicide – and the local robin acted like a bird gone mad.

His attacks were non-stop, the beak's frantic probes hurt and the rival robin had to concentrate purely on defence. Twice he was bowled over, righted himself with a flurry of wing beats then he had had enough.

With his feathers awry he launched himself into the air and flew a wobbly path away from the tree. The ditch was long. There would be another suitable place on its bank. He would set up home in the next territory. If the other robin trespassed *there* he would have the legal and moral right to act like a mad bird. As it was, right now, by the chestnut tree, he knew the law was against him. The robin *had* staked his claim first. Right had been on his side – to say nothing of superior might.

The local robin flew into the tree, perched, and burst forth into a victory song. His red breast puffed and heaved with emotion as he poured out his glory to the creatures below.

The hen flew over and perched near him, suitably impressed and more than prepared now to accept a courtship if offered to her. The cock robin swelled with pride and glory and the tree was happy for him.

As the air warmed and the spring season became permanent other creatures stirred into life again. Usually at some time in the winter the hedgehog would awake and, cautiously, appear for a brief stroll.

The weather though had been so severe that during the past months he had stayed deeply hidden in the ditch among some roots. Leaves, twigs and dead grass had made an ideal nest the previous October and the winds had, over the months, whipped other debris until his sleeping place had been totally hidden. His dormant body protected against the worst of the weather, he had slumbered through the dreary weeks, oblivious to the troubles of the creatures who did not hibernate. His heartbeat had slowed and until it just ticked over enough to keep his life and the blood circulating.

The rain, sun and change in atmospheric pressure penetrated his senses. His heart increased its beat. His blood moved more quickly and the hedgehog awoke. It was a slow process which had been devised by the law to allow him to readjust gradually.

He uncurled gently, small, black tipped nose and bright eyes peeped out from beneath frowning brows. His crown and body armour of vicious spines blended in colouring with that of his surroundings.

The hedgehog was hungry which was a perfectly reasonable feeling to have after months of sleep. Wide awake he cautiously straightened and stood, one half of his body bathed in the moon's glow. He tested the air currents, ascertaining there were none around to do him mortal harm and lumbered up from the ditch to stand by the tree's trunk.

He grunted to himself and nosed the grass. It was sodden. He knew about the ants' nest but ignored it. He was far too hungry to waste time there. He must have immediate food. Slowly, rolling as if drunk, snorting to himself, the hedgehog noisily wandered along the rim of the ditch.

He found food quickly and ate well. The slugs, plentiful after such rain, were out in force. The hedgehog fell on them with glee. To wake after hibernation and come across his favourite delicacy was a real stroke of luck.

The animal gorged his way slowly down the length of the hedge. He found two worms, one snail and some tender bush roots. They all disappeared quickly into a slowly expanding stomach but still he ate on. Later in the year he would vary his diet with fruit, birds eggs and – if really lucky – a snake or two. Now though, his body demanded instant consumption with maximum protein value. The slugs were the answer.

He was a turbulent eater, very lacking in table manners, as he grunted, snorted and rumbled his way along so that every creature and bird in the immediate vicinity knew his hibernation had terminated for that season.

He heard a sound, stopped with head and body rigid and the ears flattened to its head, and froze. He scented and his little heart pounded in fright. He bolted the insect he had been eating and dropped down into a tight little ball. He tucked his head and limbs in, curled tight and waited for the danger to pass. His body made a perfect circle. The wicked spines stored out at all angles. Only the cunning fox knew how to find his body joint, insert a paw and prize him open to eat.

The badger did have superior strength in his claws to that of the fox but he was sadly lacking in guile. He shuffled past and disdained anything more than a disparaging sniff. Many a time the previous year the two nocturnal animals' paths had crossed and though their diets were somewhat similar they had never fought. There had never been reason to.

When they did meet there was food in plenty and they were both tolerant and easy-going animals if left alone to mind their own affairs. The badger crinkled his nose as he took in the hedgehog's scent but it was not as distasteful to him as that of a fox. The hedgehog smelt more of staleness from his long sleep than the downright dirty stink of the slovenly fox who considered body toiletry rather a waste of effort. Later on in the year the badger would carefully avoid the hedgehog. When the weather became hot the fleas would joyfully gravitate to the safe haven of the hedgehog spines. All creatures would then consider the hedgehog to be absolutely antisocial.

The hedgehog cared not at all. Like all members of his family he was, primarily, interested in filling his stomach. Food was an all-consuming passion only ever being superseded when it became necessary to propagate the species with a mating.

Finally, the hedgehog was replete. He slowly waddled back the way he had come. It was still a little too early for him to be awake each night. Now that his stomach was full he would return to his cosy bed near the tree and sleep for another two or three weeks. When he awoke for good he wanted constant warm weather.

He found his tiny bed, burrowed under the leaves, curled himself into a perfectly round, tight ball and promptly fell into a deep sleep.

The tree offered the protection of its boughs to another of the wild.

Although the weasel did not live directly under the massive tree's protective branches it was a constant visitor. The attraction was the ditch, bank and hedgerow. Like most of its species the weasel was reluctant to roam far from home. It preferred to obtain its food within a reasonable access of its burrow and, because of its varied diet, it rarely went hungry unless the weather conditions were extreme.

The weasel lived in the copse. It had taken over a small vole burrow, enlarged it, extended the depth of the chamber and, by lining it with grasses and leaves, had made a perfectly comfortable home for itself.

The tree knew the weasel well. It had always known it and followed it when hunting. It had admiration for the animal's fantastic scenting ability. It had deep pity for the creature selected as prey. No weasel, once on a food trail, ever desisted. Only death could stop a weasel from catching meat.

Of all the creatures of the wild which the tree knew, none was more feared and respected than the hunting weasel. The badger, hedgehog and even the fox stepped from the path of the small, red-white hunter. Such was the panic engendered by the weasel's ferocity and lack of fear that no creature of the wild trespassed near a female weasel's nest. To do so was downright suicide.

Although so fearsome the weasel was also attractive. Its elongated body moved elegantly, the steps fluid and effortless. It had the ability to freeze and hold itself absolutely motionless with just the sharp nostrils analysing the air currents for prey. It could also move very swiftly when the occasion demanded. Of all the creatures of the wild none was more dangerous than the weasel.

And the tree loved it just for this. It was so easy for the large and strong to take care of themselves. To acquire fear and respect. For such a small animal to have this too marked it out to be one superior in both courage and intelligence. A royal animal almost. Certainly one as majestic as the tree itself.

The tree though cared for all that lived under or near it. Even the humble snail was a friend not to be scorned. There were many snails in the vicinity of the long ditch but the tree had one particular snail as a friend. It lived under a stone only a short distance from the tree's trunk. It had always lived there during the whole five years of its life since it grew from the pea-sized egg which a hermaphrodite parent had deposited long ago.

Because the stone was half covered with hard-packed earth the snail had always lived in one spot. It was damp under the stone where it lay only inches from the ditch and this small site was never dry. Even when the ground lay rock-hard under the sun the soil under the stone always had moisture.

It was a large snail with a shell quite two inches high and during the winter it had hibernated. Now though it was ready to move with the rain which it loved. It never would go far or fast. That was impossible. As it took its home and its defence with it the snail had to be unlucky to be eaten.

It preferred to move at night unless the daytime rain was exceptionally heavy and humid. Its movements were wavelike from the large soft foot. A journey of a few inches was a stupendous and sometimes exhausting feat. Food was never any problem. The vegetation around the ditch and the bank was lush and the snail only had a miniscule appetite. Sometimes it would eat dead meat but its choice was always green food.

The tree's snail was now very old and the tree wondered whether it would have this friend much longer. It had nearly exceeded the lifespan allowed by the law. Many of the snail's brethren only lived for two years. By those standards this snail was ancient. It had been fortunate not to succumb to the hedgehog or numerous other wild animals for whom the shell was a mere irritation to be cracked with only slight pressure.

The snail had been lucky to survive from the birds' attacks for so long. Because its home was under the stone it had lived in such safety for its long life. Few knew of the small cavern on the stone's underside. The wind was forever blowing leaves and dead grasses in that direction. The entrance was constantly blocked off from view.

Creatures like the foxes never bothered to glance under a stone unless driven to desperation by starvation.

As the other creatures came and went the snail stayed close to its stone. Because it had been there for so long the tree had become attached to it. It knew this relationship must end and, perhaps, very soon. Everything had to finish and die. Only the tree itself lived on and on, for ever and ever. The tree was constantly forced to make new friends because none of the creatures of the wild could live so long. It was a harsh fact. It was even a necessary one. It was the simple law but it meant the tree was solitary in every way and clung to the fragile friends while it had them.

The sticky buds had swollen with the milder weather. Each small scale, a replica of its neighbour, was now stretched to the limit. Any day now the buds would split open and the delicate green leaves, all twisted into a cone, would be free to unfurl and stretch themselves into new life.

The grass too was responding to the mild and dampness. Under the shadow of the tree it was still stunted with short blades. Away from the branches' great umbrella the grass was moving upwards. It was sending more blades through the soil. These extra blades allowed the wet to linger longer which, in turn, promoted further growth.

Even for late March, it was unusually warm. The tree wondered if this weather was really fortunate. After such a savage winter it might have been better for spring to approach just a little more hesitantly. This rapid transition from cold and dry to warm and mild was unhealthy. All green matter might outgrow its strength. The wild creatures, especially the earth animals, were still in their thick winter coats. If though they started an early moult and the frost came back they would be miserable with cold.

Only the tree itself was safe. Its armour of bark was thick like steel plate. Impervious to seasonal weather temperature. Its new leaves would be another matter. Right behind the growth of the leaves were the flowerbuds. Sudden, unexpected frosts would perform havoc and mean that, in the autumn, there would be few chestnuts for the animals and birds to scatter around.

The tree's own reproductive cycle could well be endangered. It was with some relief that the tree saw the weather change again, not to the drastic frosts of weeks ago but just to a cooler environment more in keeping with the time of year.

The west wind had vanished. Instead, air currents blew more from a northerly direction. The temperature dropped and growth was halted for a brief period until the wind changed again.

The law had realised that all was going ahead too quickly and that made for a dangerous situation. Life paused and waited once more. Only the hardy flowers thrived in the hedge bottom, the snowdrops and wild violets were impervious to weather changes. They were made tough and only grew where they would be sheltered against the most inclement weather.

The whites contrasted violently with the violets and this again was what the law had decreed. Apart from providing seasonal beauty these vivid white and purple colours were sufficient to attract any early bee who might live in a nearby hive. Thus pollination of these cold weather flowers was ensured.

The nettles, vicious with their stings, were

highly vulnerable to frost. They halted their growth, then waited for balmy weather to arrive permanently.

The birds carried out nest building but more as a perfunctory gesture than active homemaking. It was far too soon for eggs to be laid and young chicks to be hatched. Such delicate new life would quickly die in the cold. Also, the birds' natural diet of insects would be unavailable.

Only the burrowing animals went ahead with birth preparations. The rabbits' warren hummed with activity as does prepared their nests and the bucks kept to themselves away from the nips and thumps of mothers-to-be who had other matters more important to attend to than tolerate the irritabilities of bucks.

There was a constant coming and going as grasses, leaves and other soft materials work were collected and taken to the various nesting chambers. The chief buck rabbit was in a state of nervous alert while these preparations took place. Once the does had vanished to their chambers he would be able to relax his vigilance a little. He knew perfectly well that the vixen had a litter of cubs. He also knew that his arch enemy, the weasel, had produced young. Of all the animals it was the weasel he feared the most. There was nowhere out of bounds to a weasel. The vixen, at least, could not get into the warren and it was rare for the foxes to dig. Only the badger was a miner that way.

The tree oversaw it all. The problems of the multifarious life underneath its umbrella of the branches, half brown and half green now. The utter complexities of the various animal, bird and insect species as they went about their daily lives, only made the tree realise all the more acutely that it was solitary. There was no other giant like itself for miles. What chestnuts did drop beneath the umbrella and try to root were only smothered by the parent tree. It was a form of genocide, it was also just another law. The chestnuts must be carried to another area to root and grow. That way two giant trees would not be in constant competition for the vast amount of nourishment needed for survival. *That* way propagation was more successful for the species.

CHAPTER FOUR

The vixen introduced her four cubs to the outside world in April. She chose her time carefully as she selected dawn. A lovely spring dawn when the mist still clung in tendrils of white froth around the hedges and ground, broken, here and there, by the early sun.

It was still. The birds' dawn chorus had not yet commenced. The nocturnal animals had retreated to their dens for their sleep and the day animals had not yet made an appearance.

It was that in between time, neither day nor night. There was no breeze or sound. Every leaf on the tree was immobile; everything stood and held its breath.

The vixen appeared first. Her sharp face and bright eyes peeped from the earth's entrance. She stood frozen. Her senses screamed warningly alert for any kind of danger. She scented the air, listened, then reassured, stepped forward daintily.

Four red balls of fluff wriggled after her.

Sixteen little paws scratched the damp earth as eight black eyes blinked nervously in the unaccustomed light. They clung to the vixen, unsure of themselves but encouraged by her presence.

It was also big and wet and white. So vastly different to the snug haven of their underground den. The cubs were not sure they liked the transition from dark, dry warmth to this huge, glaring open full of strangeness.

The lone female cub squatted, looked at the vixen and wailed a protest. Two of her brothers promptly copied her. The third male cub, the smallest, did nothing but look around in astonishment and curiosity. This cub was the outsider of the litter. The vixen had soon learned that fact. The cub was ready to fight for his fair share of the food but he often missed out because of his inherent curiosity. While he considered an event the other cubs would sneak in and steal that which was meant for him.

The vixen might snarl and nip but to no avail. The outsider was always left out. Because of this he was small and already lacking in muscle and strength. His curiosity though demonstrated a high degree of intelligence. If this could be utilised he would make his mark. If not, he would stay small, weaken and die. From being just an outsider he would become the runt of the litter. It was the law that all runts and weaklings die. Apart from the fact that there was no place in the wild for them, the law decreed that the weak must never be allowed to perpetuate a species. The law demanded that only the best should live and breed.

The vixen sensed that a cloud hung over this male cub and already she was starting to lose interest in him. The next few days would be touch and go. They would spell the difference between life and death for the outsider.

The old dog fox watched his mate emerge with keen interest. He stood, showed himself, advanced a few paces, then halted. His brush wagged gently. His mouth was half open, red tongue lolled while his eyes sparkled. He wanted to approach nearer but he knew his place only too well. Any vixen with new cubs was a tetchy animal. He waited to be invited.

The vixen, in her turn, regarded him a little balefully. The cubs were hers. She had borne them in pain in the bowels of the ground. They were her pride and joy – except the outsider. The dog fox might be the sire – he might even be the meat provider but, as yet, she was not too keen to share her cubs. Also, she was a little uncertain of her mate's reaction. Would he be jealous? Would he harm them?

She snarled softly. A snarl which combined threat and warning. A sound which brooked no opposition to her will. The dog fox heeded the snarl. He sat, then lay down and waited quietly. He was older, wiser and more patient than the vixen.

The cubs were afraid of this huge animal who faced their dam. They had correctly interpreted the vixen's snarl. Their whole attention was riveted on the dog fox. That he happened to be their sire was incomprehensible to them – and also irrelevant. That he was a bringer of meat was also unimportant. They were still too young and too small to appreciate good, red flesh.

They huddled obediently by the vixen's side still very unhappy at being in this great, white unknown. They much preferred to be back in the comforting darkness of their earth.

The outsider cub suddenly decided to ignore his mother. What was that creature over there? *Why* was he there? Why did his mother snarl? The smallest cub could not appreciate that the other animal was himself many times larger. He was consumed with curiosity. He must, he simply must know what it was!

He waddled forward, eager to discover for himself. The vixen let him go without protest. He was the most unimportant of her brood. If there had to be a sacrifice made, he would suffice. He could be the experiment.

The small cub stopped when two paces from the dog fox. Now he showed his intelligence. Even though eager to explore further he scented for danger and debated this situation.

The other's scent was friendly and warm. The cub advanced and gingerly touched noses. The old fox's tongue shot out and the cub found himself being licked enthusiastically.

What a bold cub this was! A small one but not a frightened animal huddled near his mother – and the dog fox licked his cub again with pleasure. He nuzzled the red ball of fluff while the cub tried to dodge the large tongue to reciprocate his own friendliness. The cub was full of sudden happiness. He felt at ease with this large animal. Dimly, his instinct told him that this red creature, so big and powerful, was part and parcel of himself. Curiosity satisfied he flopped down and nestled comfortably between his sire's paws.

The vixen had watched this confrontation with great attention. Reassured she now advanced slowly herself torn with two emotions. Enormous pride with her new family and total jealousy at the outsider's obvious preference against herself. There was a savage – but brief – internal battle then her maternal instinct won.

She reached her mate, touched noses and paraded the rest of the family for inspection. It was a happy occasion. The tree was glad. It had seen similar meetings so many times before but never had it watched such an unusual cub. This one, this outsider, was a replica of his sire far more than the rest of this litter.

It was not just in colouring or make or shape either. It went much deeper. There was a great intelligence. A power which rose above basic instinct. Later this cub would demonstrate his cleverness with guile and deep cunning. Attributes so necessary for an animal like a wild fox. This cub, this outsider, would either die quickly or grow to maturity with a power and inherited wisdom which would assure him long life and good hunting.

This small, insignificant cub, was the prince of fox cubs.

As the tree was the focal point of the ground animals so also was it the hub of tremendous bird activity. There were many starlings in the copse and frequently they flew to perch on the chestnut tree until its branches were alive with speckled birds.

The flock of starlings nested amicably in the copse's trees with homes made from carefully selected grasses, twigs and moss. Already some of their hens were sitting on eggs, as was a blackbird who had her nest lower down in the hedge from that of the robin.

The cock blackbird was a glossy coal-black with a bright yellow beak. He stood out in this vivid colouring against the more dowdy brown plumage and lemon beak of his hen who kept more within her home confines.

All this activity in the tree infuriated the robin but there was little he could do about it but hurl abuse. He objected to all birds who constantly crossed his territory and when they actually perched on *his* chestnut tree the red bird's fury knew no bounds.

Both blackbird and starling were considerably bigger than the robin which fact made a direct assault pointless. The little bird had to content himself with an aggressive display of open truculence, which left none in doubt as to where his true feelings lay.

The robin though was not quite as guiltless himself. He also trespassed when he thought he could get away with it. The female robin had laid five buffy-white eggs, each a freckled replica of its neighbour with light red spots.

The cock robin was frantically busy finding food. There were some insects appearing but not enough for two adult robins. So he was driven to hunting for worms and indeed anything capable of being swallowed.

The rival robin, long since recovered from his defeat, had staked out his territory further down the hedge. He had flown around his boundaries and proclaimed he had taken possession with a song. It was common knowledge that area of the field was taken.

The chestnut tree's robin though sometimes sneaked over the frontier when seeking food. The soil down by that section of the ditch was very muddy and the worms were so easy to find there.

Such a mission was, of course, fraught

with extreme peril. To trespass was offence enough. To be caught in the act of taking another's worm was the most heinous of crimes.

The tree's robin was caught one dawn. He had carefully scanned the other's territory and, unable to spot its legal owner, he had made a swift foray into the forbidden zone.

He probed the mud and caught the tail end of a slow retreating worm. He leaned back, fluttered his wings, and heaved. The worm fought for its life. For a few seconds it was stalemate. Then the tree's robin gained a precious half-inch. The worm stretched but was finally forced to yield.

Out of the blue, retribution struck with violent force in the shape of the territorial owner. This robin went berserk with rage. How *dare* any other robin trespass and steal his food – let alone the chestnut tree's robin.

The guilty robin hastily released the worm who, seizing the chance of a lifetime, shot into its burrow with frantic tail wriggles. The worm was bruised and battered but, at least, still alive and not a robin's breakfast.

There was a brief battle between the two robins again before the tree's robin surrendered. He knew he was the guilty party. He had no excuse and with this knowledge he lost the battle.

He flung himself into the air and fled wildly back to his tree to sit, feathers ruffled and out of order, to recover his battered masculine dignity. He was so upset that it took him a good five minutes before he could muster enough breath to drill a song of defiance to match the victorious robin's anthem of triumph which floated so easily through the air.

The tree accepted these fights as part of life and just another aspect of the law. For all wild creatures there were only three basic and primeval possessions. A mate, food and territory – not necessarily in that order. It depended upon the season of the year and the weather.

All the creatures though, whether bird, animal or insect, understood that life as they knew it could not proceed without these three important needs. For these, they would fight and die. Of all the birds who used the tree as a friend none was more aggressive than the little robin.

At night the tawny owl was a welcome visitor to the tree's top branches. This was a friend with a very different character and temperament. He would appear in utter silence and drift to a branch from which its marvellous eyes could discern detail on the blackest of nights.

He looked bigger than he was with his fluffed-out feathers. His large head with ruffs of feathers around big eyes which radiated out, gave the bird an appearance of being in perpetual shock. His colour of red-brown with a red-white underside blended perfectly into the night. He was almost invisible.

The small nocturnal rodents on which he lived rarely knew he was around until they were snatched helplessly in his claws.

The owl's nest was in the trunk of a rotting tree which, struck long ago by disease, offered the perfect home. The bird liked the chestnut tree. At night, even when the moon failed to shine, he would perch on top of a branch and sit in utter silence and stillness. His remarkable eyes could penetrate an incredible distance. Woe betide any creature that moved if it were small enough for the owl to lift in the air.

He could fly quickly. His great eyes would rivet on a blurred movement. Large wings would span open and he would swish through the air, plummet down and snatch his dinner. His hoot of triumph was mournful when it shattered the night's silence. It was also a death dirge to those little night animals who lived in the area.

The tree understood the ghoulish hoots. Every creature, big or small, must have the pleasure of proclaiming victory by one way or another.

Towards the end of the month the weather changed again to become balmy. The tree's leaves were fully open now. The white candles of flowers – almost an inch across – were attractive, especially to the bumblebees who were busy pollinating as they prepared food for their hive.

The hedge was a mass of gorgeous colour, mostly bright green but broken, here and there, with the startling white flowers of the blackthorn which preferred to flower first and produce leaves last in direct contrast to its neighbours.

Green grass had come in profusion. The whole of the countryside was a rainbow of fresh colour. With these warm, sunny days the creatures of the wild thrived. They had already forgotten the miserable winter.

It was in this lovely weather that the tree greeted another friend whom it had not seen since the previous autumn. The adder too lived in the copse in a burrow under old logs. She had a mate who lived nearby and who joined her for breeding.

She was a large snake as adders go, being two feet in length, but her colouring, although not as bold as the male adder's, was vivid. On her flattened head the two dark lines crossed into a startling V. Down the length of her body was a black zigzag line to terminate in her stumpy tail.

Her poison fangs were carried in her upper jaw. They folded back into a neat position when her jaws were closed. When opened the two poison fangs dropped into an automatic striking position. Like all of her kind the adder was timid and, if left alone, would always hasten from an encounter with a foe.

To the mice, voles and moles she was a most terrible danger. To all the birds nested low in the hedge she was as perilous as the weasel. The adder loved eggs. She delighted in the young birds preferring them even to frogs and lizards.

She was not yet ready to give birth to her living young who would be as perfectly formed as herself – even down to the poison fangs – but she was hungry and attracted by the sun. She slithered elegantly out to the short grass under the tree and, for a while, basked happily in the sun. She was a reptile who craved warmth and she would do nearly anything to get heat.

At the adder's appearance the two robins froze. The hen was on her nest, the cock on a tip of a hawthorn bush. They knew that any slight sound would only draw them to the adder's attention and with eggs in their nest, disaster would be inevitable.

They did not appreciate that the adder was not fully awake after hibernation. She was content to sunbathe then find herself some mice. Later, when fully active, she would soon seek out all the young birds she could.

The tree welcomed this friend back and draped its branches over her protectively as, finally, the adder gracefully slid back into the copse. Each scale moved against the ground, gripped and gave the reptile motion. The adder would be back again to sunbathe and the tree waited.

With the wonderful weather of wet and warmth the wheat in the field began to grow rapidly despite the poor topsoil. A thick, green carpet hid the earth and provided a playground and a hunting site for the animals and birds.

The rabbits revelled in the wheat's growth.

The tender shoots were succulent and in such abundance that it was well worth the travelling distance from their warren.

The grey squirrel and his mate also made continuous forays into the field when she gave such a perfect cover against predators.

Of all the animals who moved to the field none liked it better than the hare. The female hare had produced three leverets in the open. Now they were old enough to be moved she had deposited one leveret at a time in forms, preselected and well separated from each other. Each form was in the large field and now that the plants' shoots were so high only occasionally could the hare's black-tipped ears be seen moving above the wheat as she travelled from form to form.

The leverets were ready for danger from birth. Each form was a small hollow which the female hare had painstakingly scratched in the earth. In these the leverets crouched. At the slightest suspicion of danger they would freeze back into the ground. Their brown and fawn colouring blended into the earth so that, until they moved, they were quite invisible.

The female hare fully understood the precarious lives her leverets led. She never approached any form direct but would lope along in the general direction, then pause to sight and scent for danger. She would rise on her hind legs and look over the wheat. Once sure no fox or weasel lurked in the vicinity she would cross over to the form in great bounds and always at an angle. Thus, no direct scent trail was ever laid to her crouching leveret.

The hare did not like the copse. It was too closely confined with trees and under-growth. She would feel stifled there. She was a creature of the wild, open spaces. She never even visited the tree because the hedge corner where the tree stood was considered by her to be too cramped. The ditch and the hedge corner could hide too many enemies.

But the tree knew the hare and watched her in the distance. She was a good mother and ready to die for her young. She could box with her front paws and the kicks from her powerful hind legs were strong enough to make even a fox dodge aside.

Her major defence was her speed and ability to keep going but always she liked to run in a circle. Even though she roamed a larger area it was still nothing but a huge perimeter with the tree as a focal point.

As the wheat grew so her forms became absolutely hidden. At the same time, the leverets had abundant food to hand. They were animals of the open and scorned holes and burrows so the leverets' senses were highly developed from the day of their birth.

They greeted life with open eyes, an acute scenting ability and most of all, sharp hearing. Their large ears caught every sound in the air while their sensitive feet understood each ground vibration. They had thick coats, ready for any kind of weather and were tough animals.

Even with all this though, they were still an easy prey to the fox and weasel. Their lives were fraught with dangers which the burrowing animals were able to avoid in tunnel or chamber, but they survived.

The hare had many forms in reserve for occupation by a leveret if the original form was discovered. There was no hesitation on the mother's part. She would take the leveret by the scruff of his neck, bound away with him and place him in a fresh and undiscovered form. She was continually on the move and in a state of nervous alert. She slept in short bursts but always her huge ears were checking the air like radar antennae. Although the weasel could, given time, run her down to the point of utter exhaustion, and the fox crush her life into nothing with his powerful teeth, both enemies first had to capture her because her whole existence depended upon never being wholly at rest.

The law was finely balanced on its scales. It could never allow one species to succumb to another and be wiped out. Although many leverets were eaten, enough lived to reproduce their kind and those who did rise above such tragedy were supreme animals. The most perfect of their kind.

CHAPTER FIVE

The tree was able to watch the cubs in May. It noted the differences in their behaviour and character. Most of all, it studied the behaviour of the prince. The prince because he was no longer an outsider.

The vixen brought her family into the space beneath the tree to play very often now. They had grown and were eating an all meat diet. She chose dawn and the quiet time of the late afternoon. The dog always had meat for them and the prince's new tactics showed his superior intelligence.

After going hungry for two whole days the cub had learned. He still had the same insatiable curiosity, this he would never lose, it was as natural to him as breathing. He adapted himself – to stay alive. When the vixen gave them their food he rushed up, seized a portion then retreated to investigate it and satisfy his inquisitiveness.

The first time he did this he was challenged. His sister and brother cubs ate their meat, turned and saw his untouched. They charged en masse, hell-bent on theft.

The lone cub stood and faced them. His paws straddled a portion of meat. He flattened his ears, drew back his lips and snarled. Every hair on his back rose and quivered with rage and defiance. The other three cubs skidded to a halt and stood then they milled around him uncertainly. They wanted his meat. They did not though, fancy daring his teeth.

The solitary cub suddenly understood that, small as he was compared to them, they were afraid of this display of fury. He continued to snarl and rumble while he lay down, both paws firmly anchored on his meat. He had learned the most priceless lesson that those who show they can fight for their rights will gain immediate respect.

The cub sniffed at his meat, pawed it and finally, in slow dignity he ate. The others watched him with slavering jaws. None studied him more than the vixen. She was impressed with his spirit. When each meal brought a repeat performance the vixen started to regain interest in this cub. He was no longer the outsider of the litter. With his fair share of meat he soon caught up in strength and weight.

The cub also acquired confidence. He

plunged into the mock battles that the cubs held. He learnt to duck and weave. His reflexes sharpened. He was already fields ahead with his intelligence and this was soon coupled with cunning.

He found that the others were in awe of him. He was the winner of nearly all the single combats and even when two cubs ganged up on him they had their work cut out to roll him over, belly up, in the posture of submission.

He was a tangle of red fur, heaving body, boxing paws and flashing needle-sharp teeth. He was a force to be reckoned with. He did not learn his power immediately. It only dawned on him very slowly that if the other cubs were afraid of him he could use their fear against them. *He* could take *their* meat.

The first time he tried this was late one afternoon when the dog fox returned with three field mice in his jaws. He dropped them down then retreated to lie near the vixen, panting a little from the heat.

Three mice. Four cubs. The animals could not add, they could not even understand quantity. But they did realise that their sire's offering was not enough to go around. Four cubs charged for three dead mice. The prince was first and he left customary investigation until later. He shouldered one cub sideways, butted another with his head and nipped the third on her shoulder. The female yowled and retreated hastily. Her two brothers turned round ready for a frontal attack to seize the mice.

The prince dared them. He snarled. He rolled his eyes. He flattened his ears, puffed his chest out and made enough threatening noise for a dozen cubs. His display of arrogant defiance and rage was not all show. The other cubs knew, by now, the force of his teeth and temper. They could charge from all sides. They could steal the mice that way – but was it worth the price they would have to pay?

They snarled back. They whined to the vixen and danced around the defiant cub in their humiliation and anger. He ignored it all. He kept up his one-cub show of wrath while he sniffed and investigated his prizes. Then, slowly, as was his custom, he ate them all. One after the other.

Neither vixen nor dog interfered. There were plenty other mice to be caught and every litter of cubs had to acquire a hierarchy because nothing was more sacred than meat.

So the prince became the boss-cub. But

only where his contemporaries were concerned. His power went to his head and he foolishly forgot himself and defied the vixen.

Now the cubs were older the vixen sometimes went hunting with her mate leaving the cubs safe in the earth's chamber. The other three cubs were quite content to wait in the dark's familiar safety until their mother returned and gave them leave to join her under the tree.

Not the prince. He was ready to go out with the vixen and the dog. Already he was jumping to explore, investigate and learn more about the great open which was filled with so many enchanting scents and sounds.

He left the chamber and padded softly up and out under the tree. He was intent on following the vixen. Because of his youth and inexperience he was clumsy and noisy. He trod on a twig which echoed through the quiet morning air. To the cub, it was just another interesting noise. To the vixen a hundred feet away, it was a shock wave of danger. She whipped around and raced back to the tree ready to do battle for her cubs.

She leaped through the hedge corner and, instead of some animal intent on killing her cubs, she was greeted with the boss cub sitting down debating which trail to take.

The cub sprang up to greet his dam but the vixen's wrath knew no bounds. She jumped forward and nipped the cub's quarters unmercifully. The cub yowled in astonishment, shock and anger. He turned and instinctively bared his teeth. The familiar snarl rose in his throat. Only too late did he realise this was the vixen and not one of the other cubs.

The vixen nipped him more sharply, once, twice and three times. The cub fled, brush drooping. He flung himself back down the tunnel and into the haven of the dark chamber. He shuddered and shivered but he also learned. He had to obey and conform still. Boss-cub he might be with the others of the litter. With the vixen he was a mere nothing.

The tree understood and approved. The cub was intelligent, he should not need two similar lessons. He must obey the laws, his dam's and the wild's governing law. That was how it had to be for survival.

The tree was in full leaf now. The days of May were seasonal, damp nights and sometimes wet ones but with sunny days. Not the roasting sun of summer but a gentle warmth which filled everything with a desire to produce and grow.

With its branches fully leafed it had provided a thick umbrella of shade which kept the grass beneath short and thin. The ground was usually dry because little rain would seep through the thick canopy of clustered leaves.

There was constant action now in the tree from the highest leaf down to the base of the trunk where the ants' nest bustled with activity. The ants had taken longer to move from the sluggish and dormant winter state but now, fully awake, they hummed with activity. Food was their constant thought. The precious supply of aphid eggs had long been used up and they had scouts out all day hunting in various directions for news of an aphid colony.

They were slave-keeping ants. It was imperative that some aphid eggs be captured. They would then be brought into the colony and carefully tended until hatched. After that they would be kept as slaves in a well-constructed pen with walls of the earth. The great attraction was the honeydew secretion from the lesser insect.

The intelligence found in the ant was as great as that displayed by the fox cub. The economy of their elaborate community with its well-disciplined workers exceeded that found in the foxes' earth. In some degrees the ants' memory was superior to that of the fox. Their ability to communicate with each other certainly equalled that of many of the higher animals.

The ants also displayed a high degree of unselfishness when it came to a fellow ant. They would help him, succour him and feed him. In return for this close comradeship the ants had to be able and willing to give their all to the community without thought of individual reward.

Everything that happened was done specifically for the benefit of all. Only the great queens were above such mundane matters because they were of the blood royal. They had the supreme right to the best and the first choice because for the queens nothing was spared. They had their servants who would work themselves to death for the giver of life. They groomed the queen. They fed her the choicest morsels. They removed her eggs with tender and loving care. The whole colony revolved around the queen. Without her there was no colony because she was the be all and end all of life.

The tree's colony was old and large; divided into countless passages and chambers.

Because of the size of the colony there were a number of inert queens. Great insects whose sole production was the millions of eggs in their lifespan which could go up to ten and even more years.

Once laid the precious eggs were moved about from chamber to chamber depending upon the temperature. They were constantly licked and after sixteen days in warmth the young hatched into larvae to be fed half-digested food before turning into pupae.

What class of insect would later emerge would depend upon the original food given. This, in its turn, would be governed by what class of ant the colony required. More workers? A queen? Or males to fertilise a queen on her nuptial flight? It was a complicated way of life governed by the law.

A colony could rarely have too many sterile workers because they were expected to work themselves to death for the benefit of all. It was their calling. Their place in life. This they accepted because it was the law.

For the males there was the brief period of being flattered, fawned and honoured until a queen was ready to take to the air to be bred. Once a male had performed this vital task he was no longer required by the colony. He must die. He had served the purpose for which he had been bred and now he was of no further use.

An ant would eat anything though the preference was always for something sweet hence the everlasting quest for aphids and their sweet secretion. Any ant who found a nest of aphids would hurry back to the column and inform the inhabitants with gestures, touches and little foot movements.

Immediately the news would be sounded and a battalion of workers would line up to march off under a leader. Each ant was disciplined. Each knew his duty. Some would milk the aphids there and then. Others would take captives back to the colony. There was never a dispute over who did what. Life was too short and hectic for argument.

All the time the soldier ants would be on guard against larger insects and hostile ants who, in turn, were looking for live booty in the form, even, of cocoon ants from another colony.

War was never declared. It just happened. Let a foreign ant wander near the colony and he died instantly under the weight of the guards. Let the foreigner escape though and that was another matter. *That* ant, in turn, would inform *his* fellows and invasion might well take place without war. No quarter asked or given. No holds, of any kind, barred.

Their intelligence and the ability to communicate with each other was always demonstrated if two separate ants found two piles of food of different sizes. They would return to the colony and ask for assistance. The ant who had found the larger pile of food would take the greater body of workers. While the ant with a smaller find would take a lesser number because nothing was wasted. Certainly not the energies of workers. There were always far too many jobs for them to be doing at all times to have excess workers to collect a small find of food.

Perhaps the most favoured workers, if such a way of life did have any form of favouritism, were the nurse workers whose life's work was to tend the eggs and the young. This they did with devotion and pleasure. It was perhaps the best worker's job but there was never any trouble in who should be a nurse worker. Every ant's position in life had been pre-ordained before it reached maturity and the ant had not yet been born who would consider questioning his status in life.

Although aphids were the favourite slaves the ant also captured beetles and kept them in pens, well fed, to be used later as food.

There was no waste as there was never internal strife.

Of all the creatures, great and small, who lived under, in, or with the tree, none had such a perfect communal way of life as that of the ant. The smallest, the weakest and, perhaps to a casual observer, the most insignificant.

The tree knew better. These tiny insects were great friends and also helpers. They would attack invading caterpillars which might damage the tree's precious leaves. They would destroy fungus and bark-spore disease and so the most humble helped the most high and mighty and demonstrated, yet again, the wisdom and justice of the law which made a time and place for everything which was understood and acceptable to all.

There was colour. Colour for beauty and colour for a purpose. The yellow of the celandine, buttercup and dandelion. The blue of speedwell and bluebell in the copse. The purple of woody nightshade, the white and blush pink of the sweet-scented hawthorn blossoms.

There was more colour in the air as butterflies now appeared. The dainty orange-tip came and the cabbage white with an early tortoiseshell. At night there were moths, large and small, beautiful and drab.

All melted into the law's pattern. The colours to attract the insects to pollinate. The great variety of the flowers' colours was also part of the pattern. No one species of flower was ever pollinated more than the other because certain insects and butterflies were only attracted by particular colours. Nothing was left to chance. No opportunity for perpetuation missed.

Another came. She flew in from foreign parts and landed on the tree. She was, indeed, a little later than usual but her instinct had told her about the severe winter and cold spring. She had delayed her journey until sure of the weather.

She came paired up and was ready to lay her eggs. The tree wondered who would be the unfortunate parent birds to be compelled to adopt the bandit cuckoo. Would the small robins be pushed from their nest? Or would a starling lose her chicks?

The cuckoo though did not care for the area near the tree. There were too many birds who mistook her hawk like appearance for the real thing. Twice she had been mobbed by smaller birds so she had no real inclination to tarry.

She had a single purpose of mind. To choose a suitable nest and lay her egg in it to be hatched and the nestling reared by foster parents. It was such an easy way to continue her species. She did not really like the country. She much preferred the hot climate but the law dictated she laid her eggs in the temperate zone. Her chick, when hatched, would ruthlessly kill the chosen nest's other inhabitants to obtain the sole attention of two unselfish foster parents. He would grow big and strong then, later, depart after his unknown mother. He would have no guide to take him across the seas but he would arrive at the preordained destination quite safely. The law had ensured that navigation was inherited.

The cuckoo did not stay. She soared from the chestnut tree and the smaller birds stilled their songs and activity. She looked too much like the dreaded hawk but the tree was glad to see her go elsewhere. The robin's nest was a favourite site for the cuckoo to choose and tiny robin chicks would be totally helpless against a huge cuckoo nestling.

But the law believed in variety. It made freaks. It organised weird animals. It went in for them in the colours and downright shabbiness. It was never boring and only very rarely did it make mistakes. When this happened and the law realized, the species would be doomed to die. Their food source might disappear by disease or drought. The mistake might even become sterile and the line finish that way. The law was delicately balanced but, sometimes, it liked a macabre joke. The behaviour of the cuckoo was one of those rare happenings. The cuckoo was the law's laugh.

By the end of May all the young for the season had been born or hatched and were adjusting to life in the wild. None, though, led a more precarious life than the rabbit. The fully grown rabbit had enemies enough. The youngster was lucky to survive at all. Many does, with a litter of four or five, failed to produce a surviving animal. Because of this, the law decreed that they be prolific breeders and that they be taught, in their very young days, the constant danger of just being alive.

The teaching fell on the doe. Near the tree, to one side of the main warren, a doe had raised a litter of four and every day she had them outside. They played but it was a frolic in earnest. Again and again the doe went through a ritual with her young. By constant repetition she taught them to follow the white flash of her tail as she ran from them back to their burrow.

Once her young had understood the doe introduced variations which were pure instinct. She would run, the young follow, then she would leap aside at an acute angle. To start with, the young rabbits were baffled when the white tail they had been following so faithfully vanished. They halted in consternation. The doe repeated the trick. She went through the same movements again and again until the young had learned that the object of this move was to fool a chasing predator.

The white tail was so distinctive any chaser would follow. A sudden sideways leap and the white tail vanished leaving the quarry baffled. Not for long – but giving enough time for a desperate rabbit to reach the safety of the burrow.

There were so many enemies. The fox and weasel were merely two. There was constant peril in the air from the daytime hawk and the night-time owl to whom a young rabbit was a succulent meal.

The buck rabbits were harsh to their young. They were rough, cruel and aggressive enough to make the young live in fear in their own warren when the bucks were about. The does were in a constant state of submission and would rarely stand up to a buck rabbit in defence of their young.

On the bucks' side was the appallingly noisy, dirty and overcrowded conditions of the warren. The males were responsible for safety. They could rarely relax outside, and inside the warren the bedlam of noise frayed their nerves and tempers. It was a vicious circle brought about by the underground city.

It was possibly this very reason which, many thousands of years ago, had driven the hare to live above ground. A harsh life in the open was one which was clean, sweet smelling and full of freedom. Although still closely related to the rabbit the hare despised its relative. Like the badger, it was clean and fastidious. To the hare, the rabbit stank! The two species avoided each other by mutual consent and the hare's record for rearing its young was higher than that of its slum-dwelling cousin.

It was one of the peculiar situations found in the wild where disgust and loathing existed between related species.

On the last day of the month tragedy struck when least expected. As it had so often in the past the tree witnessed it all and could do nothing but watch in silence. It was obvious what was going to happen. Only the victim was unaware of its impending doom.

Out of their five eggs the hen robin had only managed to raise three chicks. Two of her eggs had been infertile. Like all the other parents in the wild they were constantly on the go seeking food for their clamouring young.

The robins had to eat their meals in hasty snatches. They were continually harassed. They were overwhelmingly tired. This was all inclined to make them a little careless. They had little energy to devote to being on guard which was understandable even if foolish.

The weasel also had her family to feed. Her youngsters were only a few inches long nevertheless they demanded red meat and plenty of it. The creatures of the wild were extremely wary now. They knew the weasel had young. They also knew her ferocious temper at the best of times. They really feared her now – so the weasel had to work hard to find food. When this failed, as it sometimes did, she resorted to guile.

On that particular afternoon, the weasel was desperate to take some kill back to her young. So far, her efforts had been totally unsuccessful. She knew the robins' nest was in the hawthorn tree but it was high and well tangled in among the sharp spines.

The hen robin had just fed a large worm to her chicks. For a minute's rest she descended to a lower branch which, though, was still three feet above the ground. The weasel spotted her and, without hesitation, picked up a fallen leaf, tossed it into the air and sprang after it. The leaf fell, the weasel chased it and threw again. She repeated the show and totally ignored the robin but every leap after the leaf took her nearer to the robin's twig.

The hen was astonished and hypnotised by the sight of the leaping weasel and tumbling leaf. She remained fixed to her twig, head to one side, her bright eyes staring in amazement.

The weasel leaped again. The leaf soared high, the bird watched – then it happened. The robin saw her danger but too late. The weasel sprang but not after the leaf. She shot straight upwards in the air and aimed for the robin. Straight as any arrow the thin body arched and savage teeth latched in the hen robin's breast. The little bird gave one pathetic squeak and died. The weasel fell back to the ground, the dinner safe between her teeth at the identical moment the cock robin returned with three fat, wriggling grubs safely clutched in his beak.

The cock bird took in the situation in a flash. He dropped the grubs and flew at the weasel in rage. The weasel ducked. She had no intention of letting her prize go. At the same time she knew the cock robin could do her no harm.

The robin swore and buffeted the weasel with his wings. The situation was hopeless but he had to make a gesture at least. The weasel glided away and the robin flew on to a branch. For a few seconds the little red bird knew grief but then it was gone. There was no time for such emotion. The hungry chicks were screaming to be fed. The robin flew down to the grass, found the grubs, pecked them into another neat pile and flew up to the nest.

From now on the little bird would have to work twice as hard and fly twice as far. He had lost his mate but the chicks must be reared while one parent lived. It would be hard – but life in the wild was always severe. The hen robin had relaxed and paid for her stupidity with her life. It had been a basic law that fools must die. Only the best were allowed the privilege of life. Whether the cock bird could succeed and rear the family alone was another matter. So many factors had to be considered. Would the weather be normal and the usual insects abound? Or would food become scarce if the weather turned unseasonably cold? If the latter, the robin would have to travel further for food which would exhaust his slender strength.

Without him the chicks would certainly die. They were nowhere near strong enough to leave their nest. The robin had to stay alive. Whether he died after that was, almost, immaterial. He would have done his duty and kept the law.

CHAPTER SIX

The June weather was appallingly wet and miserable but, with humidity, the plant life thrived. The wheat grew thick and tall. The nettles, docks and campions fought each other for space along the ditches' bank which soon turned into a minor flood as the ditch choked.

It was miserable weather for the vixen. She did not sleep in the earth now during the day. The cubs were far too boisterous. They gave her no peace despite snarls and threats. She hunted at night, as did the dog fox, because their young had voracious appetites and were forever hungry.

The vixen had thinned down. She was gaunt, constantly tired and edgy as she moved from the earth and sought a daytime bed in the bank above the ditch where she was away from the cubs but could still keep a wary eye on their safety. The flood water even drove her from there. She retreated into the copse which instantly worried many of the lesser creatures. The vixen herself took great care not to make her bed near the weasel's nest.

The cubs resented being left alone but knew better than to leave the earth's safety without consent. Even the prince cub was now extremely wary of the vixen. It was not just respect for her teeth but also for her flashing temper. The more relaxed dog fox was also feeling the strain of hunting for so many mouths. He looked at the rabbits' warren and considered the easy meat there but it would have been both lazy and criminal to kill so near to home. The time had not yet come for the emergency rations to be used.

The dog drove his body out each night in relentless pursuit of anything that moved and could be eaten to try and fill the cubs' stomachs. The vixen was on the same perpetual quest.

Once both animals had been a lovely shining red but their colouring had dimmed with over-work. They were completely ungroomed, their rib cages showed as they sacrificed themselves for their cubs. As fast as they hunted and brought game back so the cubs clamoured for more. Their appetites were seemingly insatiable. The three cubs fought together increasingly in the earth.

Only the boss cub remained aloof and above such common affairs though even with his dominance over the litter he was never quite full.

The tree knew the pattern so well. Soon, very soon, the cubs would leave their earth. They would have to undergo a brief lesson in hunting for themselves and, once this was over, they would be on their own. The gaunt vixen and haggard dog could not keep going much longer.

It would not be long before the vixen became bored with this domesticity. She would do her maternal duty for a little while longer. She would not desert her cubs until she was sure they would survive on their own but her teaching would be brief. The cubs would have to assimilate learning instantly. They would get no second chance. The law had decreed that hard-working vixens must recover their strength. To do that they had to be alone again; to live and hunt just for themselves. It was a sensible law because it thrust the young cubs out into the wild and taught them to stand on their own feet and acquire confidence before the winter came.

The tree would then be alone. The earth empty once more, but it was a good earth and never stayed empty for long. The four cubs would go their own way but the tree was sure that one would return. The obvious choice would be that animal with the most dominant character. The strongest cub who, more than the others, regarded the earth where he was born as his personal possession. Of all the cubs born in that earth none had shown such qualities as the prince cub. The tree knew he would come back.

Where the vixen would go was not known. Vixens were a law unto themselves. As the more valuable sex, to be wooed, fought for, and won, the selection of the maternal earth was always theirs and theirs alone. This vixen might even come back the next spring but, it was more than likely, she would go elsewhere. Her territory covered a huge area with innumerable earths, holes, tunnels and drains.

In the middle of the month the heavy rain ceased and the vixen allowed the cubs out during the day. She had no need to teach them caution. They were born with that. While she rested the cubs played together and started elementary tracking by trying to follow each other but, as yet, they had little body scent. This would not come until they left the earth. It was a simple omission the law allowed to protect such young animals

117

while they lived in the earth.

The cubs explored the large area around the tree's trunk where the grass was constantly short and stunted. There was so much to see and learn. All the other creatures had to be tabulated into various sections in their brains for instant recognition and understanding. The intelligent learned quickly. The stupid slowly. Later on, the intelligent would feed royally, the stupid would go hungry until they did learn. It was up to them. The law had no time for fools.

As the cubs' confidence increased the vixen allowed them to stay out of the earth for a longer period. She also gave them their freedom at night while she hunted. The cubs would not, she knew, roam far and they had sense enough now to run for the earth's safety should endanger arise.

The cubs loved the night. It was their natural time because they were nocturnal creatures. They were so much at home in the dark. The blackness was their friend and ally. They started to roam in the copse and through the corner of the wheat field, but they were always highly alert. The slightest sound halted their activities until they were able to ascertain the source of the sound. Whether it was friend or foe.

They had enemies. Not many but they were still small and lacked the adult fox's strength. They also had to learn the wiles of their neighbours. Who could they defy and chase? From whom should they turn aside?

The prince cub learned easily and quickly but not always painlessly. His curiosity, so highly developed, led him into far more trouble than the other three cubs combined. He was also a loner. He disliked the others now that they feared him. He detested being followed. He insisted on finding out for himself while keeping his own company.

It was probably rather unfortunate that the first animal the prince encountered should be the hedgehog. A very hungry hedgehog, intent on nothing but insects, worms and, most of all, delicious slugs. A night wanderer in no mood for argument or delay.

The two met in the centre of the copse. Each came from an opposite direction. They rounded the bend of the trail and halted abruptly. They were both rather shocked at seeing each other but it was the hedgehog who recovered his wits first. He could see the cub was still very young but any fox could mean trouble. He dropped his head forward, tucked in his front paws and rolled

119

into a neat, tight ball with every spine sticking at right angles.

The cub had heard the hedgehog's strong snuffling approach and knew he should have turned aside or run for safety from this unknown. The other cubs would have done this. Such action went against the grain with him. He *had* to find out what made such a strange noise. Curiosity and fear were entwined together as the cub gingerly approached the circular hedgehog.

He inhaled the unusual scent and registered the picture of the tight ball. For the rest of his life that smell and sight would translate into hedgehog.

The cub walked around in a circle. He was both baffled and intrigued. He stretched out a paw and gave one hard, experimental pat then recoiled sharply and yipped with pain. Little blood droplets appeared on his pad. The hedgehog's armour was sharp and lethal.

The cub was annoyed. He circled again, wary and alert. His sharp eyes noted the position where the hedgehog's body joined in a circle. He tentatively patted the join with his other front paw. No pain! Nothing! Emboldened he pushed a little harder and his claws slipped into the body joint. By chance, at the first meeting, he had discovered the way to break the hedgehog's defence. No spines here meant no pain to himself.

If the cub had been a fox the hedgehog would have died, there and then but this was only a cub. An unimportant creature, still wet behind the ears. It was rare for the hedgehog to be presented with such a unique opportunity. Too often he and his kind were at the receiving end from the fox. Now that his defence had been breached he had nothing to lose and a revenge, for past sufferings, to be gained.

The hedgehog opened his small jaws and with tiny, but very sharp teeth, bit the cub's paw – hard.

Again the cub recoiled and this time he yelped with pain and shock. The hedgehog seized the opportunity to lumber away on more important matters like filling his stomach though he kept a wary eye on the cub and, more important, he listened for sounds of an angry vixen's approach.

The cub sank back on his haunches and thought miserably about his sore pads but the lesson had gone home. Hedgehogs could only be approached from one direction. They were not the easiest animals to over-power because of their vicious armour, but they were not invincible either.

Whereas the other cubs would have hurt themselves by repeated and even prolonged frontal attacks the prince had assimilated the lesson with the minimum of pain himself.

He turned to limp back to the tree. The haven where he never received pain or shock. Halfway through the copse he heard a new sound. A harsh one which rattled and echoed through the still, night air. He forgot his pain and instinctively dropped into a silent stalk. His movements through the copse's thick summer undergrowth were delicate and quiet. The vixen had not taught him this. It was natural. Something handed down through generations of wild breeding as an essential to survival.

The sound rattled the air again, harsh, violent and hostile. It came from the tree and the cub's hackles rose in apprehension.

He poked his mask through their hedge's twigs and stared in amazement. The animal making the noise was the same size as himself. He did not appear dangerous so the cub stepped forward and stopped three paces from the tree's trunk.

The moon broke through the clouds and the badger's white striped face glowed in the light as, once again, he stood, stretched and clawed at the tree trunk. His claws rattled and bits of bark flew to both sides. The tough tree was ideal for the badger's purpose. His claws needed frequent sharpening. They were in constant use as tools and weapons and the fussy, precise badger liked them to be really sharp. Satisfied at last, he dropped and deigned to look at the cub.

They stared at each other. Younger, uncertain fox and confident, unafraid badger. The badger's lips curled disdainfully as he inhaled the powerful fox scent and dirty body odour. He stepped forward and the cub blocked his path unwittingly. It did not occur to him to move because he could see nothing to be afraid of in this animal. There were no sharp fangs or raised hackles. No snarls or other threats – so the cub stood his ground. After all, it was his area. This was *his* home.

The badger, like the hedgehog, recognised the cub for green youth. A creature far beneath himself in importance. He strode forward and, seeing the cub had no intention of moving, went straight. The cub curled his lips in bold warning then the badger had reached him and swung a paw forward in one powerful blow. It landed on the cub's shoulder, swept him off his feet, and parted the skin letting blood well up. The claw was razor sharp.

For the third time that night the cub cried with pain and shock. It was not that the cut was deep or even painful. The cub cried from humiliation and utter loss of dignity. The badger shuffled away. The cub watched him go acutely aware that he was still very young. His confidence had been shattered. It had been a most disastrous first night alone. One day he would be strong enough to stand up to any animal. Right now, he wanted the vixen. He yowled again.

The tree understood. It was the ancient cry of the young for a parent.

The vixen responded and burst out into the clearing. She had heard both cries even at a distance and had immediately turned aside from the game trail she was on. The last plaintive wail had pushed her into a gallop.

The cub came flying forward to receive sympathy. The vixen caught both hedgehog and badger scents. She growled, then licked her cub and reassured him while the tree stood guard protectively.

The other cubs rejoined the family gathering, a little awed by the boss cub's deflation. They inhaled the tangled smells and, from them, they too learned that such scents now meant battle.

It had been a constructive night which none of the cubs would ever forget. They had all acquired lessons which would normally cover many explorations.

The boss cub was not deflated for long. His spirit was too strong and vital. His curiosity was unimpaired but, from now on, he would be ready for anything. His guard would never be down and he would attack first at the slightest provocation. Once he was fully grown he would be a formidable match against even the grown badger because he would never forget the treatment he had received which he had done nothing to deserve.

The tree had seen many sights in its long life. It too had sympathy as it rustled its branches overhead. The badger had often sharpened its claws on his trunk. Over the years, as it grew tall, there were many jagged slash marks in the bark. Once, it too, had been hurt by such wounds. Now it was far too powerful to feel them as, one day, this young fox would be too strong to be awed by any badger.

The rabbits, deep in the bowels of their warren, had heard the fox's cries. They lay still, frozen with fear despite their deep safety. They had little defence against the fox if caught in the open and the cries had told them the vixen had given her family permission to leave the earth.

They shivered with worry, none more so than the buck rabbit who ruled them. They all knew the law and its rigid application. They were reasonably safe having their town so near to the earth – just as long as the foxes were adult and complied with the law.

Cubs were another matter entirely. Any young animal, their own included, had no sense and lacked all knowledge of the law's code. If they gave them a chance, the young cubs would certainly hunt them, even if only to exercise their speed and tracking ability. It was more than reasonable to suppose that some of them must die under the cubs' fangs until the law about not killing on the doorstep was understood by them.

Who was doomed to die? Which one of them? Buck, doe or youngster? They could not stay in their warren. They had to eat which meant going out on top to face what-ever might be waiting. There could be no holding back when dawn came.

The buck rabbit now had to prove that he was worthy of the title he owned. Warily, every nerve alert and whisker a-twitch, the buck poked his head from the main burrow and stared around.

It was a still morning with just the birds singing at the rising sun. There was a gentle breeze from the west which rustled the tree's leaves in soft, harmonious background music. The air was filled with a multitude of sweet perfumes from flowers, leaves, grasses and the earth itself. This was a moment of truth for the rabbit. He cautiously hopped out, took a quick look around then sat up and stared hard for any enemy. He inhaled vigorously. No fox, no weasel – everything appeared to be safe. He hopped further and a doe daintily followed his example. Emboldened, the rest of the warren's inhabitants followed suit. They were hungry and started to graze.

The buck rabbit was uneasy. He did not know why. Something kept prodding at him. He could sense trouble but he could not understand it. All appeared to be well. His instinct though was correct. Ten minutes after starting to eat trouble appeared in the shape of another buck rabbit. An upstart of a younger animal whom, often in the past, the leader had punished, usually for no particular reason than that of asserting his position and authority.

The younger rabbit knew the time and place to challenge for the crown had come. He had reached full strength. And does were so sweetly attractive – especially those belonging to the leader.

The two rabbits eyed each other. They gave little grunts and snorts and stated their intentions and assessed each other's abilities then they exploded into action. The younger animal bounced forward and the older rabbit met the charge with two well-aimed kicks. Little tufts of fur flew in the air. The does watched with great interest. The young rabbit winced under the kick but he was made of stern material. He let fly with his hind legs in return. For fifteen seconds both rabbits bounded around each other and kicked furiously. Their long claws churned, sending white and brown fur flying. Then the younger rabbit had a stroke of luck.

He was speedier than his rival and he took a chance. He deliberately left himself open for a kick, saw it coming, dodged it and kicked out himself with both powerful hind legs together. The blows landed on the elder rabbit's ribs. The aim had been accurate. Two ribs immediately parted in a fracture and the old leader flopped down in pain and defeat. The younger rabbit prepared to kick again. The older animal knew he could not take such another blow. He flinched aside and, in so doing, acknowledged defeat and the loss of his crown.

Highly delighted, the young rabbit, the new leader, bounced around then pranced towards a delightful doe who, seeing the malicious look in his eyes, turned and fled for the warren. The buck chased her. The whole of the town's inhabitants were galvanised into a flurry of action. Within seconds, the area was devoid of rabbits.

Except the loser. He was in pain. He was maimed. He was doomed – and he knew it. There was no place left for him now. He would be unwelcome in the warren because the old and sick were never wanted. He dragged himself towards a burrow long left empty because of its dampness. A refuge – any refuge – was what he must have. He was nearly there when the dog fox came upon him purely by chance.

Both rabbit and fox spotted each other at the same time. The rabbit emitted a pathetic squeal of fear. The fox bounded forward. He gave one practiced slash with his sharp teeth and the rabbit died instantly. The fox pawed the rabbit's still body. He was not hungry, neither was his mate nor the cubs. There was abundant game for all at this time of the year. He had killed automatically without thought or hesitation. If he had come across ten similar rabbits he would still have killed them. He could not help it. It was part and parcel of his make-up. The law had given him a ferocious blood-lust coupled with a rigid drive to kill when red meat should appear whether he was hungry or not. It was this inflexible drive which helped to keep him alive in the lean winter months. It was simple law.

The fox turned and stalked off. The bloodied body slowly started to stiffen and immediately gave out a smell from the quickly rotting internal organs. The insects joyfully followed the smell. The gases increased as the sun arose and the flies appeared. What a find! A body, with stiff blood and fur! On this beautiful carcase they would lovingly lay their eggs. The more it stank the better they liked it. When the eggs hatched their dear little, white grubs would have enough rotting flesh – the best – on which to live until they could safely pupate.

The ants, beetles and worms also hurried to take their share of such a rich booty. By the time they finished there would be precious little rabbit left. The birds and wind would flutter away the skin and fur. In a short space of time it would be as if the buck rabbit had never been.

The law would not tolerate waste or untidiness. Everything that lived had a purpose but once that ceased to exist the remains could not be allowed to despoil as litter. They had to be removed but, in so doing, they must also be of use to others. Apart from being clean, tidy and energetic, the law was also thrifty.

During that month the tree lost another friend and also gained a rare visitor.

The snail had been restless and often left his stone to eat the rich green plants which grew around the bank. Travelling was a laborious effort and the most the snail could manage was an inch per minute but the snail had travelled and eaten its way for well over a yard one particularly damp evening. The vegetation was lush and satisfying.

As the snail travelled it could not help but leave a white trail of mucus in its wake. It was very bad luck on the old snail's part that two predators were out that night and that, slow as he did move, he was spotted by both.

The hedgehog picked up the mucous trail at the identical moment the tawny owl swept casually overhead. The hedgehog shuffled forward eagerly. The owl swooped. Both were so intent upon their find that they almost collided with each other.

The hedgehog had a shock when the moon disappeared under the blanket of the owl's broad wings and the owl had to bank sharply to the left to avoid impaling himself on the vicious spines. The hedgehog recovered his wits first. He lumbered forward the necessary six inches, grabbed the snail between his little jaws and crunched. The snail withdrew into his shell but it was a forlorn gesture of defence.

A row of sharp teeth cracked down, the fragile home splintered and he became a tasty titbit for another. The owl hooted his loss, flapped wildly over the hedgehog who had reverted to his defensive ball, then banked and flew off for a more lucrative victim.

For the first time in years the stone was alone. The tree sympathized. It knew what loneliness meant. Perhaps, one day in the future, another snail would discover the stone and see what a desirable residence it was.

The toad was such a rare visitor that the tree could not believe its luck when the creature flopped lazily out of the damp ditch to sit on the grass and await some unwary insect who would wander by. It was a very large toad and unlike its close relative, the frog, it disliked constant water, unless mating in the spring. The toad's brown-grey colouring merged well into the gloom of the night. It sat quite still, only heaving flanks indicated it was alive but it was also highly alert. Its tongue shot out and captured an insect. The toad gulped then resumed its stance. It took a lot of insects in one night to satisfy a toad's appetite but, by dawn, the toad was relatively replete.

Now it turned to hide from the day's glare. It retreated back to the ditch looking for a hole or damp place without actual water. The tree watched the great hindlegs propel the creature from view as it disappeared between a dock and a dandelion. There it would stay hidden until the next night. Only the tree knew its secret place and the tree was never treacherous to its friends and neighbours. It loved them all too much. The good and the bad. The kind and the cruel. It was the centre of their life and they were the axis of its existence. They were all part and parcel of the law's great plan for life.

CHAPTER SEVEN

By July the tree knew the exact mood of the winter to come. It had been covered with a profusion of flowers but only half of these had set into nuts which were still tiny and hardly distinguishable from the fan-leaves.

The last winter had been severe – almost without precedent and now the law decreed the cold months to come must be more lenient. Everything that lived must have a breathing space to replenish stock and gain strength. The winter to come would be mild and green. Vast quantities of nuts would be wasteful because the animals would have no need for them. They would not starve and the tree itself needed time to regroup its resources and to recover from the toll taken of its roots during the savage months of January and February.

The wild understood this news. Many of the lesser animals mated again to produce a second crop of young. The does in the warren were particularly busy. So many rabbits had been decimated when there was no food their species must be replenished in force.

The same bulletin had been received by the birds some of whom had laid another clutch of eggs. The wild dog roses in the hedge threw a sweet-scented cloak of pink flowers intermingled with the hawthorn's bright green leaves but there would be few hips and hardly any haw berries.

The ants also received news but they ignored it. They were such busy creatures that they prepared for a cold siege by a pure instinct alone. The aphids were out in force and scout ants travelled forth each dawn to locate suitable colonies for innovation and capture. The precious aphids' eggs were taken back to the nest and put into storage for winter consumption. It was out of the question for an ant to be idle.

The same applied to the bees. Workers were in the air with the first sun and they drove themselves until dusk in their quest for pollen to make honey. They too had no intention of wholly believing the news. If the weather did become savagely cold again and their hive lacked honey they would die. Astutely, they worked as hard as usual. If the weather was kind they would have excess honey in their hive's combs but it would not be wasted. They would raise more young, even extra queens, and perpetuate their kind by letting the surplus queens go and start a hive elsewhere. Many bees had starved to death during the last winter when the honey supply had dwindled to an all-time low. They had deliberately withheld themselves from food so the mighty queen should not go without.

It was hot and sultry, uncomfortable weather for everything. The animals and birds were listless, only moving during the cooler parts of the morning and afternoon. The plants and grasses wilted and even the great tree acknowledged the atmosphere with drooping leaves.

There was some coolness under the tree's shade and the cubs spent a lot of their resting time either in the copse or near the tree's trunk. They scorned their earth now. That was a place for babyhood and they were nearly adult.

A spider had taken up residence in their old home. It was a perfectly ordinary garden spider of the female sex and the dark burrow was considered an ideal place for a web.

The spider arrived on the wings of the wind one beautiful dawn and realised the potential of the earth's mouth. She alighted daintily and immediately prepared to home build. At the end of her abdomen was a spinneret which resembled a watering can's rose and from here she proceeded to spin the silk for her web.

An internal gland in a muscular envelope contracted like a syringe, the liquid silk was then forced down and out through the duct as she spun her silk. The instant the liquid silk hit the air it hardened and became manageable. The spider had the ability to alter the thickness of each silken strand depending upon its place in the pattern of her web.

She made herself a safety drag-line then, aided with the air currents and by her own light weight, she crossed backwards and forwards over the earth's mouth, upwards and downwards until, at completion, she had a regular and beautifully patterned web.

She then hid herself near a thicker strand which would act as a communication cable. She had considerable patience even though still young. This was her first summer. Out of the many eggs her parent had laid she was one of the few survivors that managed to escape the attention of the birds, lizards and other enemies.

She had hatched as a perfectly formed miniature of an adult and implanted in her was all the inherent knowledge of the architect which the law decreed she and her kind must have from birth.

The position was perfect. Many insects flew around the shaded area of the tree and her delicate net was constantly embroiled with the struggle of some frantic insect who realised its fate too late.

The humid weather suited the tiny insects and the spider hardly seemed to have to take a captive back into her hiding place before the alarm sounded yet again. She killed quickly and efficiently with her jaws and so well fed was she that she was able to make adequate provision for the winter months to come. She too did not quite believe the news that the law had decided on a mild winter. It was better to be safe than sorry.

The vixen knew. She also believed. She was heartily glad because the chains of domestic love had started to wear very thin. Almost as thin as her temper. The overpowering and fiercely protective love she had borne for the cubs was gradually being replaced by utter boredom with them and their antics.

The time was rapidly approaching when she knew she had to be alone again. She had started to crave for solitary freedom to live her life with only herself to consider. She had nearly done her duty to her cubs. Soon they must stand on their own feet. There was very little more she had to teach them. Already they could track and were fully conversant with the wiles of hunted game. They had learned how not to be puzzled when a trail ended abruptly but to cast around in a large circle until they discovered where a hunted quarry had leaped sideways to baffle them.

Their bodies told her they were nearly adult. Their scent glands were working now they had left their birthplace for good. She only had one trick to teach them but, as it was of prime importance, she could not take her freedom until this final lesson was understood and assimilated without question. Until the action became automatic. She demonstrated one evening. The vixen walked in front of her cubs in a straight line and carefully placed each hind pad in the exact spot vacated by the front one.

This was essential for the cubs to learn. When tracking a highly elusive quarry under difficult conditions, when meat was scarce, it became urgent that the hunter keep his eyes solely on the game. The paws must fall automatically into place without the cub looking down twice. He had already glanced down once to make sure that a dry twig or piece of brittle ice did not snap and reveal his stalk. To repeat the movement was stupid and could result in the meat being lost through distraction.

The cubs did not really need the lesson. That action was inherited to a certain degree and they were soon polished and skilful, able to move through the copse as silently as the adder in the undergrowth.

The vixen knew she was free. At last! She could go off on her own and wander as she chose. She would only have to hunt for herself. She wanted no company but her own. She certainly did not want the dog fox. He bored her almost as much as the cubs. He had served his purpose to her as she had to him. They had reproduced themselves. Now they were free to live as they liked until the next mating season drew couples together again.

The tree understood. It had witnessed many other separations in the past and it wondered if it would ever see this vixen again. She would roam far and wide and cover miles of ground in sheer pleasure in being self-contained again. Whether she would ever return to this earth to breed again the tree knew not. It was not likely. She had only been brought to this particular spot by the wiles of a cunning dog fox who loved this area solely because he himself had been born here so many long years ago.

Vixens were peculiar creatures. Utterly devoid of sentiment or attachment to any one place. Completely self-sufficient and wholly self-reliant.

The vixen's going was sudden. She stood up one dawn from her bed in the hedge, sniffed the air, looked at the cubs who had gathered around the tree then, without a backward glance or any other sign, walked off. She headed for the wheat field and was lost instantly by the shield of waving grain.

The old dog fox watched her go. He had sensed this moment was to hand and he too understood. He had been a good sire to the cubs but it was on the vixen that the brunt of the real work had fallen. She had earned her solitude. The older animal had no emotion at her going. That would have been unnatural, superfluous – and against the law. He too should soon feel the drive to wander at will but he was not quite ready to go. The tree was his friend, it had always been such. The area under the umbrella boughs was his home. He had brought many vixens here

142

during the course of his very long life. He had fathered many cubs. He had seen many such departures as vixens and then cubs made their own ways in life. He had not however sired a cub quite like the prince.

Between the two animals was an unusual and rare affinity. So uncommon it was almost alien. The cub and his sire were friends, and this friendship did not include the rest of the litter. Perhaps it was because the old dog fox recognised in the prince qualities which he himself had and which were absent in the others. Rare talent which had enabled the old fox to live such a long life.

They played together when the cubs still lived in the earth. Rough games with loud snarls. All the cubs used to play but it was the prince who out-lasted the mock battles. He would never give up. He did not understand what defeat meant. He had been bred only to win in a fight and his sire recognised this superlative quality which he himself had directly endowed to this one particular youngster.

As the cubs grew, acquired a sense and learned, the mock battles stopped. There were the urgent lessons in tracking and stalking but the prince cub never deserted his sire as did the rest of the litter. To the other three the dog fox had been a useful provider of meat. Now they could not be bothered with him. A fact which the dog understood and approved. It was only the law's way of ensuring that the young could leave the parental home without qualms or fear.

The prince was so different. It was his highly developed intelligence. He understood more than the others put together which was why he disdained them. He *knew* they were beneath him and he treated them accordingly. He did not attack them directly because they were, after all, his kind and the law had decreed from time immemorial that no one species killed another of its race unless battle was desperate and over the three basic factors in life. A mate, territory and food. Then, no holds were barred. No quarter asked or given. But only on these three prime factors did the law allow race-genocide.

The two foxes, young and old, were not demonstrative. Direct affection was beyond their understanding and also totally forbidden by the law except when the dog wooed the vixen to mate with her.

But they liked each other's company and, being two of a kind, they both liked the same area. Their affinity spread to the tree.

It embraced the open space beneath the tree boughs and encompassed the copse and the wheat field.

To both of them, this was home. A feeling which a vixen only had when she lived in an earth with cubs.

They would go their own ways during a night on their respective food trails but, during the day, they would sleep near the tree. Never together – but not far apart either. No direct communication passed between them in the form of growl or bark but an indirect look from their eyes spoke of their mutual regard and respect.

The tree was glad. The dog fox was a friend of so many years' standing that life without the fox would seem alien. The years though had taken their toll of the old dog fox. His speed had gone as had his reflex actions. His nostrils and then scenting ability had declined. His hearing was not as sharp and even his eyes were failing. He had been incredibly lucky to survive the last severe winter and the tree was glad that the months to come would not be such harsh ones.

The chestnut tree also liked the prince. The youngster who had been bred to take a crown of superiority over the rest of this kind. The younger animal would never want for the best vixens and the battles to come would be won for a long time because of a cunning, guile and reasoning inherited directly from his older friend. The sire had bred true – for the first time in countless litters and the tree wondered uneasily why this was so. It knew the law was wise and farsighted. Had this superlative cub come at this time for any special reason?

The prince was impatient to see the rest of his litter disperse. He regarded the earth, tree and surrounding area as his – and his alone. That three other cubs had been born there was totally immaterial. He wanted them out – and now!

The female was reluctant to go. She was a timid animal, not yet self reliant. She was happy to cling to the litter but she was as badly afraid of the prince as were the other two male cubs.

The prince made his feelings perfectly clear one dusk and ruthlessly chased the others away. For a few nights the tree watched them linger in the vicinity, uncertain and unsure of themselves but too frightened to come back and trespass.

Then their self-confidence returned and the litter split up for good. Even the timid female struck out on her own and the last the tree saw of her was a red blur travelling along the distant field, brush held horizontal. The tree knew those three would never come back. This had never really been home to them because they had been so utterly dominated by their brother cub. But somewhere, sometime and place they would find their mates and, if they survived, they would seek earths and reproduce.

The rabbits heaved sighs of relief at the dispersal of the foxes although they were still uneasy with the fact two animals remained. The old fox was now getting far too slow to catch them unless they were sick or maimed. The younger animal was another matter altogether, though he was old enough now to know the law, and leave them in peace unless desperately hungry.

The squirrel was totally unconcerned about foxes. They lived different lives with no connection. One was an earth animal while the other lived in the high, airy places at the tops of trees. They rarely met because they liked to perambulate at different times and one was a vegetarian, the other carnivorous so they never clashed over food.

The badger was disgusted that two adult foxes appeared to have taken up permanent residence in the area. It was immaterial that he had attacked the younger animal when only a cub and hurt him. Now he was adult he would have his work cut out in a fight even with his sharp and powerful claws. During the breeding season he had, like all the other inhabitants of the wild, been short of temper and ready to attack at the slightest provocation. His young had reached maturity and the urge to fight without reason had left him. He was really a timid creature of the night and was suddenly wary of the foxes.

What he really detested was the stink they left around. Their scent glands were abnormally powerful and offended him. Every track they took reeked of their passage and made him crinkle his nostrils in repugnance. He knew he could not stand it much longer. If he thought the foxes were only there temporarily he would put up with the situation but he knew, only too well, the attraction of the ancient earth. Next mating season another vixen would be back.

Now that his domestic ties had been severed with his young's adulthood the badger, though he liked the copse, made up his mind to move elsewhere. Anywhere – as long as he was away from stinking foxes.

The tree was sorry to see him go. It was a severing of a link but again the tree understood how offended the badger was. Perhaps, one day, another badger would set up home within the area but construct that home on the lee-side of the earth. The area had room for all but tolerance was necessary for species of differing habits and hygienic standards to their neighbours.

The hare was deeply concerned. Her leverets too had grown but adult foxes were a menace in the area. Although she too roamed a vast track of circular land it was all within the hunting district of any fox who had decided to take up semi-permanent residence by the tree.

Where out-and-out speed were concerned she and her kind could out-run a fox with the first burst but they had to stop for breath. Apart from the fact that this enabled the fox to catch up, the hare also knew the foxes were wise to her circular area. Why she circled she did not know any more than a fox would ever understand its bloodlust to kill for fun as well as food. They were just traits of their breeding. Habits totally impossible to eradicate.

The weasel was unconcerned whether foxes stayed or went. She lived her own life, minded her own business and interfered with none – just as long as her wishes were not thwarted or crossed where meat was concerned. She rarely had trouble finding sufficient food because being so much smaller, her consumption of meat was less and she was satisfied with smaller creatures. The mice and voles bred in such large quantities that she could, almost, live on them alone. Periodically, she changed her diet for variety but weasel and fox rarely needed to cross each other to survive.

Towards the end of that month the sultry conditions increased until the air was so thick with hot moisture it became almost too difficult to breathe. Life stilled. This was an automatic gesture of the wild whenever conditions became too much to bear. They saved their energy, themselves and waited.

The sky piled up grey and sullen clouds from the west while, to the south, huge white pillows moved across the horizon. The atmospheric pressure was charged with static electricity and life stopped. The birds did not sing and the animals huddled low. Even the insects halted their activities.

There was no wind, no air – just an un-bearable tension building up to an explosive point. Far away powerful rising currents of air within great nimbus clouds, coupled with sufficient moisture, caused instability in the sky which reached upwards to 10,000 feet. The air movements high up were violent as negative and positive charges of electricity soon started to accumulate in different regions of the cloud.

The air pressure began to rise rapidly, at the same time the temperature cooled. The creatures huddled down knowing instinctively what was to happen. The electricity reached a highly potential state and discharged in the sky. The differing clouds met and the thunder boomed, resounding and echoing in the still and quiet.

The clouds opened and hurled their contents downwards. It sheeted with rain. The water's force so strong that it came down from the sky in a thick, unbroken curtain. The drops were large and bounced on the dry earth. They splattered on the leaves making a wild cacophony of sound. They split the grasses. They smashed down the wildflowers. They decimated the wheat field.

The creatures of the wild had no understanding of cause and effect. They just knew that such things happened and they must lie low and wait. They were utterly fatalistic about the weather conditions and accepted without complaint whatever the law decreed must happen.

They were afraid though. Frightened because they could not understand and terrified because of the might and power of the thunder, rain and lightning. Even the boldest of them cowered down in a hiding place to ride out the ferocity of the sky's fury.

For many it was their first acquaintance with the supreme majesty of the sky. For others it was the knell of doom but it was not without purpose though.

Because of the decimation of certain species through the previous winter many of the small and lesser creatures had, instinctively, embarked on a vigorous breeding programme. They had not been content with even two lots of young but had, indeed, made preparations for a third litter.

Although the law had decreed that the wild must receive gentle treatment in the coming winter it could never allow the small animals to overbreed. There would not be enough food for them all. The object of a mild winter would be defeated before it commenced. So the law took a ruthless hand in affairs. It decided it must prune those who had offended.

The quickest death was by drowning. It was efficient, tidy and relatively painless.

Also, it could not be opposed.

The rain hurled itself down from an ever-darkening sky as the storm moved overhead. The noise was hell. The sound of thunder alone enough to terrify those below while the stabs of lightning were particularly frightening. The storm was the most significant event because the colossal power it demonstrated could not be matched by anything which lived.

Such was the force of the rain that the earth soon became as waterlogged as a sponge. The ditches filled and, having no outlet for the volume of water, spilled out in a flood. This was swift moving and quickly became deep.

The underground animals, the mice, voles and others, who were the major offenders, went into a state of panic. The water poured into their underground homes. Some, thinking to find refuge, followed their instincts and fled to the nesting chambers. The place of birth and parental safety. They died first.

Others tried to fight against the water streaming in but their strength was too fragile. They died next. Those who did manage to reach the top by following the uphill burrows died last because when they reached the surface, there was nowhere to go. They were not built for swimming. They tried and failed.

The rabbits suffered for over-breeding. The third litter on which many optimistic does had embarked was wiped out in one fell swoop, as flood water cascaded deep into the very bowels of the warren then rose among the labyrinth of burrows to spew out over the field.

The two dog foxes were safe but thoroughly miserable. They were as disdainful of water as any cat under such circumstances. They clung together now, they wanted each other's company and reassurance because they were badly frightened. And especially the younger animal for whom the storm was a first and unwanted experience.

The older animal was calm having lived through many summer storms but never one of such severity. He moved to higher ground seeking out a hedge position away from the force of the slanting rain. His son followed miserably. All pride and arrogance wiped from him as he huddled with his back to the storm's direction, his brush wrapped around his nose, his eyes miserable and his ears drooping.

But nothing will last forever and the law decreed that enough was now enough. The sullen clouds moved reluctantly away to wreak their malice elsewhere. The rain gradually eased and finally stopped. The flood waters started to slowly subside as white sky became flecked with the blue and then turned to gold as a watery sun appeared.

The sun strengthened her position in the sky and her rays became warmer as they pierced the damp air. Steam started to rise. White curtains drifted upwards in tendrils of frothy lace and the area took on a ghostly appearance.

The wild slowly slid into movement again as the creatures cautiously surveyed the damage and waited patiently for the flood waters to subside.

Everything was the same but had also changed. The air was clean and sweet smelling. The leaves on the trees shone with health after their soft-water wash. The flowers' heads drooped but, slowly they would lift to stare at the sun again. Shortly, once the air had lost the moisture content, the butterflies and bees would venture forth.

The stronger plants like the docks and horseradish had withstood the storm's thrashing but the nettles and weaker ones would have to send up fresh shoots. They were unable to recover and mend their broken stems.

The wheat was flat. The long stalks, with a hint of gold in their colouring, lay twisted and broken at crazy angles. The corn no longer provided a hiding place. Instead every movement could now be seen except those made by the few, surviving smaller creatures for whom the tangled wheat stalks were an immense improvement in their constant search for hiding places.

The tree was unscathed. The lightning had spared it. It was lucky. Even a royal giant like the magnificent chestnut tree was not without its foes and none was more powerful or majestic than the lightning from a thunder sky.

CHAPTER EIGHT

The creatures of the wild held a multitude of skills and trades which, if rolled in one animal, would have produced a super-breed. Their professional abilities were a combined product of the law and their environment coupled with hundreds of years' breeding and survival.

These skills were domestic, peaceful and martial depending upon the species and the situation involved. Perhaps the ant was the most highly organised with military service. Its scouts were first-class, its generals dedicated and far-sighted while the ordinary rank and file soldiers were superlative warriors. They had no fear. They never hesitated to die when ordered and often they would sacrifice themselves voluntarily against a foe much larger than themselves.

They were also highly skilled engineers as the nest proved but so were many others of the wild who led more peaceful lives.

Architecture and engineering were two common skills which were known to the birds high up in the trees down to those who lived beneath the earth. The ability to collect materials, design and build a sound and a safe home for the young was a prerequisite among many. Some, like the hare, had, over the years, found this unnecessary. A quickly scooped out hollow in the topsoil sufficed for them.

The stability of the squirrel's drey only arose from a sound design and construction. To survive the winter winds and storms at the top of a tree meant the squirrel had to build well and thoughtfully.

Some of the birds' nests lasted for many years and only needed re-lining in the spring.

Beauty was also considered. The purpose of this was twofold. To obey the law's concepts of tidiness, and the more practical idea of camouflage which often meant the difference between extinction and survival.

Although the creatures were absolutely unable to indulge in any form of mathematics some other homes were perfect in shape and size. Probably the greatest artist combined was the queen wasp. She was architect, engineer, mathematician and artist all rolled into one small creature. During the early months of the summer a queen wasp flew into the copse. She surveyed the area, spotted an empty hole near the ditch and decided it suited her purpose. She would make her nest here and immediately she set to work.

The first necessary materials were wood pulp from dried trees and dead logs or twigs. These she chewed and mixed with saliva in her mouth. Then she carefully spat this out in delicately thin sheets of paper and moulded them in hexagonal cells. Before closing each cell she filled it with one egg.

A month later the eggs had hatched to produce early workers whose first task was to assist the queen in completing the construction of the home. The queen was ceaselessly busy laying eggs in each newly finished cell so that more and more youngsters were born. As enough nurse workers had become available to attend the larvae the workers turned to the important business of food hunting for the young. They liked to eat meat in the shape of any other insect they could kill and carry. Sometimes they only rendered their victims unconscious and took them back to the nest to be kept as inert prisoners and a reserve food supply.

Now, in August, the wasps' nest was a large, thriving city with constant comings and goings from dawn until dusk. Recently eggs had been laid by the queen which, when the larvae finally hatched, would become other fertile females. Soon these females and the necessary males would take to the air to mate. The surviving female would hibernate for the winter and prepare and found her own nest in the following spring.

The wasps were fearless and vicious. When fully aroused they never hesitated to attack no matter the size of the opposition. A bee had little chance against the wasp. The bee was too civilized. The wasp too much of a pirate.

The wasp was respected. Its sting painful and, to some, deadly. The prince cub had not come into actual contact with the wasps so he had not acquired either fear or respect. Even though just about adult he still had some baby antics and would burst into sudden play and box a leaf in the air. A proceeding which the old fox regarded with mild indulgence.

The prince had started to roam though, as yet, he was content to remain within easy travelling distance of the tree. He frequented the copse often and he went to the bank less. One afternoon he felt full of energy and was disinclined to wait until dark fell before exploring. He padded along the ditch. There were many insects in the air and playfully he jumped and snapped at them. One was a wasp. He ignored the wasp's rasp of warning and had the shock of his young life when, angered, the wasp ignored the wide jaw and rolling tongue but retaliated by stinging the cub's bottom lip.

The cub fell backwards in shock and howled with acute pain. The fire ran through his lip. He pawed his lip in agony then rolled on the ground and rubbed his muzzle in the cool grass. The acid from the sting travelled merrily through his face until he felt he would explode with pain.

In desperation he fled and jumped in the ditch where water still lingered from the storm. He gained some relief but it was hours before the puncture wound ceased to bother him.

Never again, in his life, did he ever make the mistake of snapping at a wasp. He was wary of chasing any insect until he had recognised that it did not have the wasp's warning markings. The lesson was useful in more ways than one.

He remembered the coolness of the water and later used it again. Because he rarely groomed himself his coat soon attracted a host of minute fleas who burrowed down to his skin, laid their eggs and gave him untold misery with itching.

He took refuge in the water but, for the first time, his dip was unsuccessful. His head became a life-raft for the fleas and when he emerged and dried the tiny insects only moved back again to spread over their host's body once more. He repeated the dip and this time he intelligently took a small stick between his jaws. He lowered his head to the water with just his nostrils showing. The fleas had no option but to go on to the stick if they wish to avoid drowning. Once the stick was laden the fox released it, climbed out on the bank, shook himself dry and trotted back to the copse feeling free and easy.

It was one simple gesture of an animal using a tool to help himself. Other creatures had found simple tools help in their lives. A bird with a snail in a particularly tough shell would seek for a stone then slowly and methodically shatter the shell by repeated blows of the stone.

Some birds would use a large twig to help lever a smaller one into the required place in the nest. The law encouraged the creatures to help themselves in this manner by allowing the learning to become inherited in the young.

It was a hot, dry August but the wheat never recovered from the storm's thrashing. In turned golden but lay flat and the tree knew it would defy the farmer's machines. The farmer came with his noisy combines and tried, then, in disgust, relegated the lost crop to be ploughed back into the soil when the ground softened again. Thus those who hid among the corn had shelter for longer than normally allowed.

The prince loved the cornfield. To catch game there required stalking of the highest skill. The broken wheat fronds crackled in the heat. The slightest mistake in placing pad on crackling frond was sufficient to alert all game within a large area.

He became a red ghost when on the trail. His scenting capabilities reached such a high pitch that he could read the air's messages for a considerable distance. He was able to tabulate the various air smells into their appropriate sections in his brain. Once learned they were stored until required. A scent would trigger off a memory or fact, it told him whether it was meat – and if so whether easy to kill – or plant or something useless to be ignored.

The Prince was in a state of limbo during August. He felt fully adult but he knew, at times, that he still had much to learn about life. There were occasions when he was uncertain and even unsure of himself which was why he clung so passionately to the tree.

The tree represented security. This had been the area of birth, peace, comfort, warmth and an ever-full belly without effort. This was also the area where the old dog fox chose to lie for hour after torpid hour during the day. When the older animal did sally forth at night his hunting was a leisurely affair now. The frantic drive of the earlier months when there was a family to feed had been replaced by the lull – almost an anti-climax – of the gentle autumn.

Most of the wild had succumbed to this lethargic state. Their domestic pressures had gradually lessened and finally disappeared. They were free and unfettered; able to think just of themselves. Sometimes they felt the urge to play with others of their kind.

It was the law's let-down period when thin and agitated parents took a deserved holiday after rearing the young and before they commenced the rigours of winter living.

It was the time when the season's young

were flexing their muscles, learning about life on their own; exploring the great world of the wild and coming to terms with its complex laws and rigid social conduct.

Species only had social intercourse with a similar kind. To mix with others was taboo – as horrifying as badger contemplating mating with fox. During this period hostilities were at a mutual all-time low. There was plenty of food for all. Enough for each creature to replenish the strength used in the arduous breeding season. It was holiday time.

But not for the tree. The end of summer was of critical importance because the tree knew the exact number and quality of the nuts it would soon be releasing. Each precious nut was safely encased in a protective green shell which was thick and armoured with short spikes to deter the birds.

Although the law had decreed a mild winter the tree, nevertheless, had to reproduce itself and its nuts must be perfect. With a green winter to come the creatures who dispersed the nuts would be a little more particular than usual. They would only take the best. They would not waste time or energy in harvesting small or deformed nuts so the tree cut off the life-blood of sap to those nuts which it knew would not reach the necessary standard.

The stalk dried, thinned and snapped. The encased nut fell and lay on the ground to moulder and rot. It was unwanted by tree and animal alike.

It did the same to surplus leaves. Very shortly, the tree's own rate of growth would slow down for the winter resting period and it was useful now to get rid of leaves which had served their purpose. So gradually these too dropped. The creatures were aware of the tree's mood but understood it was not the pre-winter clearing of branches but a removal of surplus stock.

It was the same with the hawthorn, blackthorn and wild rose. Even the grasses were thinning, allowing the weakest stems to die so that only the best and strongest remained.

The summer flowers had gone but their precious seeds lay thick on the ground between the weeds and other plants. Some were entangled in stalks or lay and rested on areas devoid of actual soil. As the plants let-down for the approach of winter these seeds would descend too and be covered by soil. They would lie dormant and wait for the spring.

The colour of the wild had changed. In the spring it had been harsh and even vivid to attract with a speed the early insects. During the summer the colours of the flowers had softened. There were plenty of insects around now and less haste to attract with beauty. With the advent of autumn the wild's colouring became even more muted. The grass was not so vivid. The leaves had acquired a pallor which told their age. Even the bark of the tree's trunk had changed. In odd places, where the sun had reached, the bark had lightened. From a distance the tree now had a mottled and even bleached appearance. Only when the winter mists and rains came would the colour revert to the more dark copper uniform shade.

The ground was rock hard. It had been a relatively dry summer and cracks interlaced the earth except where they were knit together with the cling of plants and grasses' roots. Those who would have liked the damp and wet had vanished for the time being. Even the toad had not been seen in the open but had clung vigorously to the shaded side of the ditch where there was always a trace of moisture.

The water level of the ditch had slowly subsided until now there was but a thin layer of squelchy mud which was continually criss-crossed with tiny tracks.

Some of the tracks had become roads for mice and voles and as the route became popular among the tiny creatures, certain safety factors were incorporated into its construction.

It did not run straight nor in the open but meandered from one bank to the other. The gentle contours curved where shelter was available and took the form of a hole, burrow or sometimes just an overhang in the bank. There were cross roads and even junctions. Small areas for rest. Sections slightly raised so that the traveller could survey the scene on all sides and take general stock of the situation because it was a dangerous road on which to travel.

The bank was high above those who used the road. The grasses and weeds grew thick and tall. In them could be hidden many enemies. It was imperative that the road's users had lay-bys where they could pull in and wait should danger arise.

The first mouse to use the road did so from pure convenience as he wished to go from here to there. Others copied his trail and with constant use the track became regular and well-defined. One mouse would pause to rest and scratch a droplet of soil away beneath an overhang. Another traveller would copy his action and thus the safety lay-bys were built for the benefit of all travellers.

A mouse, more industrious than others, scratched a little burrow. Sweet roots grew beneath two large stones which lay directly in the middle of the mud and also because between the stones still lay a residue of water. Here, it was delightfully cool at all times. Others copied and a hole became a tunnel which made excellent refuge when danger arose.

Even with these precautions though, it was still a highly dangerous highway only to be used under extreme precautions. Once the grasses and plants commenced to die down and visibility improved the risk would be less but, by then, rain would have fallen and the ditch would again carry water. The road's users would have to abandon it to those who lived in water.

There were minute water fleas and one-cell creatures without the ability or instinct of the land and air creatures but who nevertheless were life even in their simple forms. One stage up from these creatures were the water bugs and beetles who lived on them.

They too had foes and so it went on. Each species had a predestined enemy. Thus the law carefully ensured that no one species could breed, thrive, grow and over populate.

Everything had an enemy. Every creature could be regarded as food by another – with, perhaps, the solitary exception of the red fox. Apart from the badger he had no wild enemy to keep his numbers down and, when it became necessary, he thinned his own ranks by smaller litters of weakly cubs who failed to reach maturity.

The whole of the wild was complex, highly organised and had been tried, tested and approved by the law. Although the creatures of the wild had no positive understanding of this they accepted with patience and stoicism the times when pruning became necessary. Any parent could feel grief at the death of the young but tears were unknown. Emotion rarely lasted for long because of the stark fact that life must go on. Death was understood and accepted by everything that lived as being, like birth, the second most natural function. Those of the wild had only three emotions which would cause them to fight to the death; the vital possession of a mate, territory and food.

CHAPTER NINE

As August had been the holiday month so September marked the start of another period of wild activity only slightly less than that of the pre-breeding season. This was a month when positive preparations had to be made for the winter whether it was going to be severe or mild.

The tree's leaves had started to change to a delicate pale-gold shade and the weaker leaves had been completely released and already lay on the earth in a thin, brown carpet which crackled underfoot no matter how carefully the paw was placed on them.

It was a sunny month but there were mists early and late which clung around the field and hedges and made the area ghostlike until the sun drove the morning mist away.

From a distance the tree looked eerie as it rose solitary and aloof with its middle trunk and branches shooting from the mist but the cub liked this weather. He could sneak up on the game which, not having his keen scent, were often baffled as to his presence.

The sunny days were warm without being too humid and he spent them lying up near the tree within easy distance of the old fox who was happily content to spend more and more time just lying around, half dozing.

By now the prince cub had met most of the wild and had learned their order in the scale of importance in relation to himself. The birds of the air were hardly worth notice. They were beyond him usually as he was too strong now for even the owl to attack.

But there was one shy and very timid creature he had not met for the simple reason that, quiet as he was, he never saw the adder. She was so sensitive to ground vibration that few could creep up on her unawares and happily she always removed herself first to avoid trouble.

On this particular day though she was hypnotised by the sun. She was not yet ready for hibernation and wanted to take advantage of every drop of warmth spilled from the sun before making preparations for the colder months to come. She had given birth to young and left them to get on with life. As pre-formed replicas of herself they only had to feed and avoid trouble. There was nothing she could do for them even if she had been inclined, which she never was. Maternal cares and domesticity were irrelevant matters to the adder.

She had come out into the corner of the field and lay in a little hollow where the ground was bare. The soil was crumbly but retained the sun's heat. She spent most of the day just lying there only, now and again, letting her forked tongue touch objects within reach to satisfy herself as to their origin.

The prince cub had also been basking lazily in a comfortable bed in the hedge. He was loath to move but sudden thirst made him get up and go for a drink. He had to walk along the ditch a little way before he found a spot where water still lingered.

He satisfied his thirst then turned, intending to go back for another sleep until it was time to hunt in the dark. He was completely unaware of the adder's existence and, if the snake had been still, would have followed his plan. But the adder's tongue moved and the prince cub stopped and stared. It was only a tiny flicker of a tongue but quite enough to take the cub's attention.

His ever present curiosity soared as he turned to investigate. The adder felt his approach and would willingly have slid off but the fox cub was approaching from the direction of her retreat to her hiding place. Baulked, the adder stayed where she was and watched with unblinking eyes.

The prince approached with slow steps, then paused to gaze down at the adder in amazement. The adder raised her head and glared back. Each creature unsure of itself and hesitant to make the first move.

The prince sat down to think about this. Ever since the episodes with the hedgehog and badger he had stifled any rash impulses to rush forward and investigate. He liked to survey the scene, probe for a weak defence, calculate the potential danger to himself and, only then, attack.

The adder appeared harmless. No spines, no vicious claws – just a long, thin unprotected body which invited the snap of strong jaws. But the prince still hesitated. Instinct jabbed at him. He was wary and he did not know why. He must be careful, that he knew but why – when there was no obvious danger?

He growled, flashed his teeth and stood to circle. The adder prepared to move but was still foiled by her retreat being blocked. The snake was also worried. The sun was on its downwards slant. Evening was fast approaching when the mist would rise and the air cool. She wanted to go. Now that the day's warmth would soon end the adder was anxious to find the seclusion of her burrow.

She opened her mouth again and nervously flickered her tongue. The prince gazed in awe at this. He stiffened to spring. He must, simply must, box at that tongue with his paws. There was still some remnant of the baby left in him.

The prince sprang, one paw striking out. His claws ready to buffet. His brush outstretched for balance. His other three legs poised as springs for another pounce in either direction. His reflexes incredibly sharp.

The adder was equally swift. The oval head plunged to the left, the poison fangs down in position for a strike. They were full of wicked venom from the poison sacs in the head.

At the last fractional second the cub changed direction. The sudden vision of the fangs had aroused instinctive danger signals. The beating paw was redirected as the fox's body jumped over the snake. The paw beat down on the adder's back in a solid blow. One of the claws was sharp. It cut, removed scales, skin and flesh – then the cub was gone. His hind legs propelled his red body to the right where his feet connected with the ground. His muscles flowed smoothly as he pivoted for another jump and turn back for a frontal attack.

The adder had not been idle. She realised no strike was possible yet so she sank her head back and down, thrust with her tail and wriggled around. Pain sheeted through her beautifully marked body where it had been beaten and cut. Hurt which made the adder's temper rise to flashpoint.

Her head darted forward in a movement so fast it was almost impossible to discern. The fangs struck. The poison ejected but the cub had gone. The poison sprayed his brush as he leapt sideways and struck out with his hind legs but missed.

Both adder and fox paused. The sun had gone, the September damp had already started to rise from the ground. The adder was dreadfully anxious to be off to her hiding place but she dare not move an inch with the fox around. Some of the poison had been used but a little still remained, enough to kill. One strike, one lucky blow was all the adder asked.

The prince flung out his thick red brush. His hackles rose. He growled and attacked again. He boiled with anger. A fury which he had never known before and which was compounded from fear as well as anger. An inherited fear which he did not understand. Here was an enemy. The greatest of them all!

He stood on his hind legs and boxed cleverly with his front paws. The adder dodged the blows while she waited the chance to strike again. She struck! Again poison squirted down the red coat of the prince's chest but his incredible reflexes pulled him back from disaster by a hair's breadth.

The adder was frantic now. It was so cold to her. The poison was nearly all gone from her fangs. A mere droplet remained in the precious poison sacs which might just be squeezed along the slender ducts to the fangs. Not enough really to kill but all the snake had left. She was almost defenceless; she only had bluff available.

The open jaws and hanging fangs had intimidated before. They must do so again. She struck and struck once more. First to the right and then the left but the fox was everywhere at once. Never still. Each jump accompanied by slashing blows and vicious jaw snaps. Each ripped scales and skin from the adder's body until she writhed in pain and fury.

The fox sensed victory. The adder seemed to be tiring and the prince knew instinctively that the reptile was anxious to retreat to the copse. Puffed with his impending victory he made a careless mistake. He stayed in one position for a tenth of a second too long. The adder struck downwards. The great fang on the right of the hinged jaw penetrated the fox's shoulder. A minute drop of the poison was injected into the fox's bloodstream.

The prince froze in shock, pawed at the wound, snapped at the adder again then jumped backwards to consider fresh tactics.

The adder seized her chance. She wriggled quickly, trying to ignore the pain from her beaten body. She must, she simply must reach her home before it became any colder. She had no poison left at all now and was utterly defenceless as well as being injured.

The fox went to follow automatically and kill, then he slowed as the droplet of poison coursed through his body. He sat then slumped as the poison fought in his blood. A great weariness came over him. His head ached and his sight blurred.

The tree! He must get back to the safety of the tree! He forced himself up and drove his weak legs forward. He rolled, stumbled and headed home. Once he tumbled and fell rolling helplessly, then he scrabbled with his legs, pushed himself erect and drove onwards.

There was the tree his tree! His home. Here was safety and peace. His steps weakened and his sight blurred – he stumbled, nearly fell again and suddenly he wanted the dark.

Where was the earth – was that it? His vision was getting worse. He must enter the earth; find the chamber, there – and only there – would he find peace. It would be like the dark womb before birth where nothing could touch him. The place where he would be fully protected and safe for ever.

He stumbled, fell, dragged himself up and lurched three more paces. It was difficult to see. There were three earths all in a row which swayed together. Which one – he fell forward and slumped on his front paws. His mask mashed the spider's web and the insect fled in fright.

The prince's hind legs clawed feebly at the grass then they found a purchase. He heaved himself onto all fours again and rolled down the dark tunnel, turned, entered the birth chamber and finally collapsed in a confused, sick and frightened heap.

He was young and healthy. He had an

excellent constitution and was bred from sound stock. The poison had been minute but, even so, the battle which now took place in the seclusion of the earth was fiercer than that fought in the field. His system was contaminated by the poison but, as it travelled, it was diluted and weakened. The strong, active heart did not falter or fail and gradually the poison started to disperse. The prince had been reprieved but all the stuffing had been knocked from his body.

The adder reached her hole and lay quietly. It had been a very near thing. There were precious few battles which any snake could survive. The field was dangerous. Only the woods were safe. She must, from now on, find patches among the trees to sun-bathe. It was going to take time for her body to heal and the winter was approaching. She had been lucky.

The fox lay low and silent. The dark of the chamber soothed his nerves while his system battled for his life. No whimper passed his lips. He was too stoical for that. He was not the vixen's cub for nothing. And from his sire the inherited intelligence started to work.

The snake was an enemy. An enemy above

all others. The danger jabs which had prodded at the first meeting had not been for nothing. They were the instinctive signals planted by the law in his makeup. He had foolishly disregarded them and nearly paid the extreme penalty in so doing.

He knew now that, given the opportunity, the adder would have left him and retreated first. He acknowledged that even he could not do battle with everything that lived and expect to win outright. He might be good – but he was not that superior.

He lay, rested and remembered. For two whole days he stayed hidden from the wild. He claimed solitude while he recovered and readjusted to the knowledge he was not invincible. He had no yearning to eat and this was normal for the wild's inhabitants. It was a simple precaution that the law took to help the sick and injured. It removed the hunger drive so the animal could concentrate on recovery.

Thirst was another matter but the prince ignored this. The effort to walk to the ditch was too much to be considered. Also, like all the inhabitants of the wild, he could not bear the thought that others might see him when not at his best. He must remain hidden. He would put up with the thirst pangs so he exhibited the wild creature's high degree of self-discipline.

The old dog fox was puzzled to start with. He woke from his sleep, stretched, yawned, scratched himself and thought about a little gentle night's hunting. Perhaps a few mice or voles. Maybe a rabbit if he could catch one unawares but nothing which required a long hunt or a fast run.

He did not look deliberately for his young companion. That was not done but he was suddenly aware he was alone, which was unusual. Although the two foxes did not hunt together they usually roamed within hearing distance of each other.

It was only when he walked out under the tree did he realise there was something amiss. His sharp senses immediately told him of unusual happenings. His sensitive nostrils picked up a strange scent and he backtracked. When he came to the spot where the fight had taken place a throaty growl arose as the hostile stink of snake hit him. He ascertained his companion's scent and blood and the ultimate in horrors – poison.

He noted the adder's track where she had slid away and he turned and followed his son's scent. He was so skilful and such an old hand at tracking that he read what had happened and understood. The soil held no secrets and when he reached the mouth of the earth he paused, listened and stared into the inky blackness.

There was no sound. No whimper. No vibration of anything alive but he did not enter. He had lived in the open and above the surface for so long that the entry into a vixen's earth would have been an unthinkable, alien move, hostile to his nature.

He did not call or show emotion. These too would have been wrong but he wondered, as he stood at the earth's mouth, his nostrils twitching, each heavy breath fluttering the remains of the shattered spider's web, whether his cub was dead or alive.

There was nothing he could do. If the cub was dead that was that. He, in the meanwhile, had to eat to live. He turned and padded into the copse for something quick and easy to fill his stomach. There was bound to be game around which lacked his wits.

The tree wondered too. It had been a rare fight and a totally unnecessary one. There was room for all to live in the wild. The fox had been wrong to drive home an attack just for the sheer hell of it. The adder had as much right to live as the fox. Neither snake nor fox were rivals in any way. They did not compete for the same food or even want the same territory. They hunted at different times of the day and night. They had absolutely nothing in common to clash with each other. There was ample room for both.

Like the old dog fox the tree was compelled to wait and wonder. Was this wonderful cub's life to be snuffed out because it had made a mistake? The tree knew the law could be harsh in its justice. This was not without purpose because severity taught the best of lessons but sometimes extreme severity could kill. Only occasionally, did the law relent to donate a second chance to an offender.

This cub with his superlative intelligence had been bred and born for a purpose. The tree acknowledged this simple fact. There had been many other cubs in the past. Ordinary, run-of-the-mill animals who bore no comparison to this particular young fox. It seemed illogical that the law could produce such a wonderful animal and snuff out his young life as penalty for one mistake – but the law was the law. The tree could do no more than wait, watch and rustle its brown leaves together in sympathy.

While it waited life went on. The birds who were to leave for hotter countries gathered and talked about the journey to come and squabbled with each other as to the best time to leave. At times, the tree's branches appeared to be alive as the birds landed in swoops and dives.

It was such common knowledge that the coming winter was going to be wet and green that the birds had delayed their departure. The tree knew that the wind must change to help them go. Let the wind come from the east and be dry and cold – the birds would hesitate no longer. In many ways the tree was anxious to see them gone. Their constant comings and goings were disturbing the nuts. Those which were ripe had started to drop, the green cases splitting with the impact on the ground but other nuts, not quite ready to leave the tree, were being disturbed too soon because of disturbances from the birds' feed and wings.

The tawny owl wished them away too. At night, the tree's branches were thronged with perched birds and there was little space, let alone welcome, for the solitary owl. His nightly wanderings disturbed the roosting birds and animosity, never far away with birds at this time of the year, soon arose. Their nightly complaints made such noise that all game froze and the owl was sore put to find his food in the tree's locality. He was compelled to go where it was quieter, where the smaller night wanderers were not in such a state of nerves from hundreds of noisy birds.

When the prince finally emerged from the earth he was no longer a cub but a mature, experienced and hardened fox. A finely-tuned animal who befitted his name. His suffering, fright and close brush with death had instilled in him a perfection of mental growth which would have taken months of wild living to acquire.

Physically, he was in poor shape from his instinctive self-inflicted starvation but it was the lack of water which had depleted his body the most. Like all red-blooded animals he could survive for a lengthy period without food but his internal organs, especially his kidneys, could not last long without fluid.

His first, weak steps took him in a meandering line to the ditch. The nearest water was still and filthy but it was water. He guzzled greedily for a few seconds then lifted his head and waited. His basic instinct warned him that it was foolish to overload his stomach with too much water after a period of dehydration. This time he heeded his natural impulses and drank in short bursts.

Once satisfied he turned to the next important action. He must have food. Good, hot red meat simply must go in his stomach and charge his muscles and sinews with strength again. He knew he was in no fit state for a long stalk and a fast chase. His need was too urgent. His meal must be immediate because of his condition.

He did not hesitate. He knew what to do. The law stated quite clearly the actions which could be taken in a dire emergency. His present condition was certainly exigent. He headed for the rabbits' warren and concentrated. At the thought of food his mouth filled with saliva which trickled from his lips. His hunger was appalling but he was too wise now to make the fatal mistake of hurrying.

His progress was silent and he approached up wind like a ghost would, belly almost flat to the ground. His red colouring merged in with the earth as he looked at the small group of rabbits eating only feet away. The buck rabbit was on guard. He was the biggest rabbit there and he would taste good. He was also the nearest and, being the leader, would be duty-bound to warn the rest before taking to his heels.

The prince calculated the distance, tested the wind once again and exploded into action. He shot forward, jaws open, tongue lolling and gave the buck rabbit the last fright of his life.

The rabbit drummed a warning with his heels and prepared to leap sideways to follow the others already running for the safety of the warren. He never made it. He had no chance. There was still much drive, urgency and sheer necessity in the fox's attack.

He died quickly as the fox killed with speed and precision. Within ten minutes he had almost disappeared into the prince's stomach and within another ten minutes his body was providing the first elements of new strength in the fox's bloodstream.

The rabbit had tasted good. The prince sat, licked his lips and felt a warm glow steal over him. Already he felt better. Another drink of water, a few hours sleep and he would be back to normal again with the resilience that always went with the young, tough body and mature mental attitude.

The old dog fox now lay twenty feet from him and the two foxes dozed in company with each other while the life of the wild pursued its normal and energetic September course.

The squirrel was hot foot after nuts now. Whether the winter was going to be white or green was irrelevant. He was a hoarder by instinct and was never fully satisfied until he had innumerable caches of buried nuts as iron rations. He was selective though. Not any old nut would do. He chose, debated and finally selected nuts of choice shape and perfect colour which told him they would not moulder and ruin the other nuts in his hidden pantry.

Sometimes he forgot where he hid the nuts, at other times he failed to eat them all by spring and the nuts would then take over and fight each other to become dainty, young saplings. The strongest nut and the one to first put down a secure root would win the battle for light and space and so found another dynasty – which was how the great tree itself had arrived so many years ago.

As September drew to a close the activity reached a frantic climax before the month of October arrived which, to the wild, was the start of what they called winter.

CHAPTER TEN

The toad had found a snug hole for winter near the bank and well above any flood line. The position had been chosen with care because there was always the consideration of a suitable site in the spring for mating and egg laying. He still ventured out for food during those parts of the day which were warmed by the weakening sun but as October progressed these excursions became less and less.

The nights were wet and distinctly cool. The hedgehog had not yet gone into firm hibernation. He still wanted to eat and store up a thicker layer of fat under his skin. During the past winter, with its severe cold, he had been forced to wake up at odd intervals to keep himself alive. At the time of the excessive frosts, when the temperature dropped very low, his heartbeat slowed to such an extent he was barely alive. He had a natural built-in thermostat and this had awoken him each time the danger depth was reached, so that he could invigorate his circulation. In a green winter he might sleep right through providing he had eaten enough in the autumn.

He had already selected a delightful nesting spot right in the middle of the hedge where there was a thick accumulation of leaves and dead twigs lying on top of fine, loamy soil. The spines of the hawthorn made a perfect barrier of defence and yet he was within easy walking distance of the bank where the slugs and snails liked to gather.

Now, he spent his last few days before hibernation roaming the copse. His hunger was insatiable, so much so, that he had even taken to hunting during the daylight hours. Which was how he came to meet the adder.

The reptile had never fully recovered from the beating she had received. Normally, she too would have taken to her winter bed by now, but her enforced convalescence of recovery had delayed hibernation.

It was sheer bad luck that she should bump into the hedgehog because the outcome was inevitable from the start. The hedgehog loved snakes but had few opportunities for catching them because he was nocturnal and reptiles followed the sun.

When he saw the adder he rolled forward and, without hesitation, grabbed the end of the snake's tail. The adder promptly struck back at him, fangs full of fresh and strong poison. The hedgehog easily countered by tucking his head down and throwing forward his visor of spines. The snake recoiled from the sharp armour in agitation.

The hedgehog had a very small mouth with tiny jaws. He usually found it quite impossible to bite any large object and, instead, resorted to chewing. He had a firm grip on the reptile's tail. With his head tucked safely behind his armour he commenced to chew a living meal.

The adder went berserk. Again and again she threw her head and fangs down to strike at her tormentor but it was impossible for her to drive the poison into the hedgehog's body. The sharp spikes stabbed at her oval head. The blood started to flow. She had soon ejected her poison harmlessly as her poor body started to satisfy the hedgehog's appetite.

She thrashed in one final paroxysm of agony with the last of her strength. She could not cry out. She did not know how. All she *did* know was a cataclysm of indescribable pain which filled her then the law took pity and mercifully she died.

The hedgehog did not even pause for breath. Steadily, remorselessly he chewed his way up to the adder's head before he stopped. His stomach was full to bursting. He could eat no more. He gave a grunt and a belch, discarded the spine pricked reptile's head and fangs, turned and rumbled back to the hedge. He was so gorged with snake it was almost more effort than he could manage to scramble into his nest. When he did collapse he fell straight asleep and the tree nodded gently over him.

The tree's branches were almost bare. Around the trunk the leaves lay thick and red-brown in a crackling carpet which, when it rained, would turn to a soft slush. Inter-mingled with the leaves were the split nut cases with, here and there, the odd nut or two which had failed to reach the squirrel's high standards. These latter might be taken by some of the birds but the tree did not mind if they lay there to rot. Enough nuts had been distributed to ensure that at least one chest-nut tree would grow elsewhere. The efforts of the spring had not been in vain.

From its lofty vantage point the tree saw everything and because of its great age and wisdom it now understood all. There was little it failed to comprehend and a small puzzle of the spring and summer slowly became painfully clear as the days progressed. The solution filled the tree with an indescribable sadness but it was powerless to intervene because it was the law.

It could merely stand in mute solitude and give the shelter of its great body while it awaited the inevitable.

The prince was restless. He did not know why or for what. He wanted to leave the area and stretch his legs in wild roaming but he could not go yet. The time was not ripe.

He was a superb animal. His stature greater than that of his contemporaries if they had dared to live near him. His aggression was unmatched. His intelligence a finely tuned instrument. He was an outstanding fox quite without peer.

Now the tree understood why he had come into being. In its infinite wisdom the law had ensured the conception of this superlative animal so that this particularly fine line of foxes would not die out. It would be up to the prince to propagate his breed in the years to come because the old dog fox was dying.

He knew it. During the summer days the older animal had slowed down considerably as everything became that much more of an effort for him. His muscles started to tire quickly. He could not run so fast nor so far.

It had been sheer hard labour helping the vixen to feed the family. The old fox had been heartily relieved to see the cubs' dispersal and the vixen's departure. He had enough on feeding himself.

He rarely tasted rabbit now because he was incapable of catching one. Instead he lived on the small animals and he was content. With less energy to expend on the chase so less food was required. His teeth were loose and mice were easy to manage. Birds' eggs would have been a tasty change to his diet but they and time were beyond him now.

The birds mocked and jeered at him in his old age but with sublime indifference he ignored them. Such pettiness was beneath one who came from such an aristocratic line. He spent many hours lying happily in the sun. It was a yellow sheet of warmth under which he dozed happily. He always slept with head on front paws and his brush drooped gracefully around his black nose. He had started to go grey with pale splatches of colour interlacing the bold red of his coat.

He was a very old fox and he had lived a good life. He could not count but he knew there had been many winters and innumerable cubs to carry his bloodline. So many vixens, so many kills, so many wonderful days free in the wild.

He did not fear death. Why should he? He had administered death hundreds of times himself. To die was as simple as to be born and it was also as natural. Death was about a long, quiet sleep where there was no want, no hunger, no cold and where peace and tranquillity were ever available.

The old fox was so wise in worldly matters. His world of the wild where all roamed free and unfettered. He knew all. He understood every season and mood of the weather. He was familiar with the lives and habits of all that lived from the tiniest insect to the largest bird. The wild had no secret from him and now, as he lay dying, it was no secret from the wild.

The king was dying! The great red fox. The mighty hunter! He lay dying.

There was an awe over the wild now because there were few who had not feared him at one time, or the other but the wild did not congregate to stare and abuse him except for the birds. The creatures' turn could come at any time. They carried on with their daily lives and left him to go in peace.

He lay at the field's edge shielded by the hedge on one side and the shadow of the tree on the other. He scorned the darkness of an earth. Those places were for vixens and cubs while he was of the open spaces.

It was a good day for dying. Cold, crisp with a winter sun, and the old fox lay and watched his world start to recede. He was not alone. The prince lay a few feet away and watched with rigid attention. He felt no emotion because what was happening was understandable. But he could not leave either. Between the two animals was a mystical link which went deeper than a mere blood tie, and which, sometimes, can be found in a species.

They were not just sire and son. They had been good friends and the younger animal knew it was his duty to stay. To watch and see the old one went to the peace he deserved.

The tree watched too. A link was being slowly severed which had been strong and genuine for so many years that the tree was humble. Mighty chestnut, giant tree, red fox – so long had the two known each other. Always the red fox had come back to his tree and stamping ground and now he was going for good. The tree would be alone again because – what would the younger animal do?

The sun started to edge down the sky to

the west. The air was crisp and cold. The night would bring the first frost. The first proper frost of the wild's winter.

The old fox lay, eyes half open looking at his wild. It was difficult to see anything now because a blur – a mist approaching – which was not the fog of night. He sensed the younger animal's presence but made no visible sign. That would not be the proper thing to do but he turned his old head and looked. He forced his pupils to clear up for the last time. He stared at the prince and his eyes bored deep into replicas of his own. They burned a silent message. They told the secrets of the wild. They handed over the sceptre, orb and crown of royalty.

The prince stared back and absorbed in those fleeting seconds all that he must know and do. He made no sound. He lay absolutely motionless. He missed nothing.

The old eyes misted over more quickly now. In a few more seconds – the old fox's eyes closed. His nostrils flared their last. The great pumping heart stilled. His head and neck went limp as his eyes gave one last nervous twitch. He died.

The wild stilled for a heartbeat of time then life resumed its normal functions again. The animals, birds and other creatures went about their own affairs. Night closed in and the tree was sentinel.

The prince stood. He felt the gap but there was no great emotional loss. This was neither the time nor the place for that. He was very much alive and he was hungry. He trotted away after game.

The tree watched him go and wondered about the future. There was so much vast country for him to explore. It was inevitable that he would soon depart. Now that the old dog fox was dead he had no tie to the area except that which came from possession and territory. Like his sire he had displayed for the tree and its surrounds a fierce acquisition against all others of his kind, even those from his old litter.

Was this feeling of ownership strong enough to bring him back next breeding season and, if necessary, fight for possession of this particular earth against an outsider? It was an interesting problem but the tree thought it knew the answer.

The next morning the farmer decided to finish ploughing the last piece of the field. The huge plough, with numerous shares, scooped up the old fox's body, twisted it, turned it and buried it back in the soil near to the hedge. By night there was no indication the red fox had ever lived.

To the worms and others whose habitat was on and under the soil, the body was un-expected treasure indeed. They would feed on this carcase until the frost gripped the earth and drove them deep down for sur-vival.

In turn, with their constant movement and burrowings, they would enrich that particu-lar portion of soil and once again the law would demonstrate its multiplicity of action.

As the air temperature dropped, many of the tree's friends disappeared until spring. The cold, wet nights with rainy days made life difficult for those who stayed active all the year around. The hedges became favour-ite places where animal and bird could find shelter from the wind and lashing rain.

The ditch filled with water and the mouse road was wiped from sight. The small rodents now made new tracks through the dead, limp grasses which afforded excellent protection which was even more necessary now. Every time they set foot outside their burrows their lives were in constant danger. They were such easy prey to others. They provided food for so many. As they were so small they were able to hide easily but, even then, their numbers were rapidly depleted during the course of one season and because of this the law was inclined to allow them to breed in great numbers.

The greatest predator they faced was the silent owl. It was not instinctive for them to look up for danger. They had to learn this. A mouse was a tasty meal for an owl. The owl would, when hungry, attack anything that moved provided it had enough strength to lift the prey to the sky. Even young fox cubs were not above attack but the fully grown animal had nothing to fear.

The owl visited the tree frequently now the migratory birds had departed. The wind and rain had removed the last of the tree's brown leaves and, with bare branches, the owl had an extensive view of a large area. Nothing escaped his eyes. A mere shadow which trembled was enough to launch the owl in flight.

As the owl was the tree's friend at night so did the robin spend more time in the branches during the day. The bird had successfully reared his family alone and, after the August recovery period, had regained his strength and sprightly behaviour. His aggression had not dimmed with time. The area surrounding the tree was still his as the piece of land further down the hedge was in the undisputed ownership of the rival bird.

They did not fight now. A mutual if uneasy truce existed between the two cock birds. They both had to survive a winter and their energies were required for this alone. Once the next breeding season approached they would open hostilities again. Now, they frequently trespassed on each other's territory without causing open conflict. They would chase each other away with verbal abuse but physical buffeting was not considered at this moment.

The wasps' nest was silent and appeared dead but the tree knew of the dormant life inside and the prisoners stored for winter consumption. The young queens and males had left on their nuptial flight and the fertile queens had found selected positions where they would wait out the winter before founding their own separate colonies.

The ants were still active during the middle of the day at the warmest peak. As they lived so low down they were unaffected by the winds. The rain hampered them. Their little bodies were unable to cope with water. One droplet of rain could batter them.

Soon though they would retire inside their

nest for many weeks and the tree would not see them. They would lie quietly, conserving body energy and just performing the most vital tasks to keep their nest functioning. The queen ant would not want. She would have the best and as much as she required no matter how many workers would starve in the process. The supply of aphids and their eggs was plentiful for a mild winter.

The tree missed the activity which it had known during the past months. Two creatures it missed most of all were the badger and the fox.

The badger's home was still and empty. The extensive connecting tunnels were no longer cleaned daily by a fastidious, timid animal and already leaves and debris had been swirled into the sett's mouth and lay in untidy piles of rubbish. These were a joy to spiders and other insects looking for dryness and winter warmth.

The tree hoped the badger would return in the spring just as it wondered about the fox.

The prince had been away for many days now but the tree knew its friend had not left for good. The fox was carefully and meticulously exploring the area adjacent to the tree. Every hedge, hollow and tunnel had been checked and classified. Should the fox's life be in danger from a source which he could neither outrun nor outfight, it was essential that he knew which tunnel led to where and how deep it was.

The prince did not care for tunnels or burrows but a degree of caution and prudence drove him to investigate everything within range of the tree. During the month of October he was in a constant state of travel and exploration.

He killed where and when he fancied and his skill rose. The first time he tried for a hare he was baffled. His speed was good but the hare easily out-distanced him. The prince was astounded then angered. He was hungry and wanted that hare. In determination he loped and it was only as familiar scenery came into view that he realised the hare had taken him in a gigantic circle.

He sat to catch his breath and think about this fact. The hare, a youngster, also paused for breath. He was badly frightened because he knew the fox was still around but he had acquired sudden confidence with his speed. The wind was from him to the fox but his huge ears caught every tiny sound. When the fox stood to pursue the chase the hare was off again. This time the prince used his guile. He noted the hare had moved to the left and now he cut across the countryside at an angle.

He used valuable hedges as cover and his gait was silent. His nostrils took into account every variation of the wind and his sharp eyes probed the contours of the land, especially the ridge and plough. He did not like open spaces and normally avoided the middle of fields but now he trotted into one and lay down in the plough. The red of his coat blended into the brown soil and, as he lay motionless, he was invisible. His brush stretched out behind with longer hairs trailing on the sides of the ridge.

The hare bounded through the hedge, surveyed the ploughed field, decided it was empty and crossed. He had no chance. The fox seemed to leap at him from the depths of the earth and although the young hare was quick, his actual body reflexes could not match those of the fox.

The prince's jaws were made of steel. His white teeth rigid poles like ivory and needle sharp at the tips. One swift snap and the hare died quickly, hardly aware of what had happened.

From a distance the tree had watched and approved the fox's tactics but it was also sad. This further demonstration had shown the fox was ready to depart. He was adult. He had explored, learned and understood everything in the locality. Soon it would be time for him to go and travel the wide spaces of unknown countryside.

That night the prince came back to the tree. His belly was full of hare. He had no need to hunt for meat for another day and night. He was replete but not content. An unease filled him which he did not understand.

This area and around where he had been born had been comforting to him. It was so familiar and friendly. It also had everything. Beautiful thick hedges full of life which also provided cover for stalking. Water in the ditch and the copse of food which provided an ever fuller larder to say nothing of an emergency supply of rabbits from their warren.

The prince was fully grown and developed. A fine, large animal whose red coat shone with health and vigour. Every muscle was toughened by constant use. Nerves, sinews, combined with the muscles, to give him a fluid gait which was untiring. He was a precise machine of elegance and beauty. A superior product of his kind.

His mask and eyes shone with intelligence and cunning. Both ears had tips of black which merged into the red-brown. His forehead was red down to his black button of a nose but on either sides of his mouth delicate white hairs rippled along his face down to a short, white shirt.

The slender but steel legs were red ending in black pads and the combination of colours merged into summer or winter colours and gave him a camouflage almost unique in the animal world because it was suitable for either nocturnal or daytime hunting.

The only unusual feature on his body arose from a thin, white line of hairs down one shoulder where the badger had split the skin so long ago. Although only a flesh deep wound their hairs had regrown cross-wise and, from a side-view, the fox appeared to have a painted, white stripe which stood out and identified him among others.

As, so long ago, badgers and rabbits had scarred the chestnut when it was a mere sapling so had the fox being branded with a unique identification mark. The tree was glad. It could recognise its friend from a great distance. It also marked him out as being different. There were very few fox cubs who had survived a clash with irate badger and lived to tell the tale.

When the prince went the tree knew the

memory of that early clash would go with him and it would be woe betide any badger who tried to cross this fox. The scar was mental as well as physical.

CHAPTER ELEVEN

Winter had been making foraging swoops across the land, advancing and then retreating as the days of October and November fluctuated between cold and mild weather.

In the middle of November the wind moved around to the east and without further hesitation, winter struck. She grasped the land and announced her arrival with a thick, white hoar frost. A frost which was totally unexpected for the time of the year especially as those of the wild knew it was to be a green winter.

The law was wise. It sent the frost as a sharp warning. Those who had not yet hibernated must delay no longer. It informed the tree its sap must slow and its roots rest. It warned the birds and others to look to their outside homes and make sure they were snug and watertight.

It told the ants to shut their doors and stay inside until spring. It warned the worms to burrow lower beneath the soil. It gave the prince a firm nudge which he still ignored.

For days he had been hunting at night and sleeping during the day in a bed in the place where two hedges made a corner. He was restless but reluctant to leave the area which was home – and his.

It was not because his friend the old dog fox had died here. That was something of the past and long forgotten. It was just a general feeling that here, in these acres, he was sure of himself and master. Out there, in the great unknown, he would be a stranger.

Unlike many others he was happy in his own company. He had no craving for any of his kind who, though they might be friendly, would also want their share of the game and the land. That, he would never allow. In many ways his character was possessive and selfish like that of the cock robin.

He was also uncertain of the reason for his restlessness. He did not fully understand the drive growing inside which was merely the culmination of his maturity and a natural sign that he was ready to seek a mate.

A vixen could not just be taken. She had to be found, approached with caution and delicacy and wooed. Sometimes this elaborate courtship, with its established rituals, took a long period of time. He might be a fine dog fox but first he had to find his mate and then win her. The winning could easily include a battle. No self respecting vixen was going to give herself to the first dog fox who happened along. The prerogative of choice was hers because she was the one to bear the young.

None of this was simply acknowledged by the prince because he was not even sure of it all. He just knew he was agitated and nervously uncertain. His mood was fragile. His temper likely to flare at the slightest provocation.

For the rabbits in the warren it became a time of particular hell. Although they had the law on their side, foxes were, at the best of times, uncertain creatures. Even if this dog fox was not hungry, there was nothing to stop him killing for fun. His fractious mood could explode at any time. Their trips for food became nightmares of hazardous travel because this fox was so quick. His reflexes and whole action so swift that it was sheer folly to leave the warren for more than a few paces. Soon, the food at hand would have gone and they would be compelled to travel further and run the gauntlet of an irate male fox who didn't recognise what his body wanted.

The tree understood its friend so well and

grieved that no vixen lived in the area. It wondered uneasily what the outcome might be for the prince if something did not give very soon. The tree's unease turned to downright alarm one cold dawn.

The prince had hunted and eaten well. He was returning to his bed for a long, lazy sleep. Because his belly was comfortably full his temper was a little sweeter than it had been of late. There had been a very light frost and mist had risen which dappled the fields and hedges in lacework.

The prince was alone. The rabbits were not yet up and neither were the daytime birds. The tawny owl had flown home to his bed. All the field mice and voles knew his habits and had prudently removed themselves until he was asleep.

He pushed his head through the thin part of the hedge preparatory to stepping out under the tree when there was the tiniest sound. The prince froze, one paw uplifted. Every nerve in his body tingled, his ears pricked and his eyes glowed with interest. As he halted so did the sound. Two small eyes glowed back at him; eyes low to the ground.

The prince gently advanced a step, lowered his head and gazed down. The female weasel returned his stare unflinchingly.

Neither moved. Both were determined not to yield ground first. The prince's hackles rose as did his tempestuous temper. This was *his* land and he, alone, had free right of passage. His ears went back. His lips curled and his white fangs shone in the dawn light as a snarl rumbled from his throat. Low, long-drawn and unmistakable in his rage and ferocity.

The weasel stood silent and completely unimpressed. She was dwarfed by the fox's stature. Her slender body was not as thick as the prince's paws but she was not afraid. She had no idea what the emotion of fear was like. She never would because, like all of her breed, she had been born without fear.

Inch for inch and ounce for tiny ounce, she was the bravest and most ferocious fighter in the world. She drew back her lips, twisted her head and showed her fangs in return while, at the same time, she gathered her body for a sudden leap to either side.

The prince was impressed. More, he was amazed. This puny little thing not only stood in his path but defied him to fight. That minute body could be crushed with one snap from his jaws. He could break the slender spine by merely resting one pad on that thin back.

The tree trembled with fear for both of its friends. It knew, only too well, what could happen. The fox could crush the weasel with one bite – but should he miss, the feral weasel would spring for his throat. Those dainty and dangerous teeth would latch into the jugular vein and nothing the prince might do would loosen them until he had bled to death. The fact that the weasel would die in the process was, the tree, knew a mere bagatelle to the weasel. She would die quite happily taking her victim with her.

For a whole minute the situation was an impasse. Neither animal could now back down without losing face and neither animal dare turn because such a movement would be instantly construed as an admission and an invitation to attack.

The animals held a tableau of hatred without motion. Just the slightest movement of the nostrils indicated they were alive. Something had to give.

Very slowly and with infinite care the prince lowered his pad. He eased it on the ground and readjusted his muscles of balance. Equally carefully the weasel straightened her head. The tree waited in acute suspense. The situation was explosive. One mistake – one error of judgment and both its friends would die.

The prince delicately moved one slow, painfully accurate step forward. Every hair was stiff with tension. Each muscle tense with nerves taut like fine wire.

The weasel reciprocated. She advanced in equal slow motion. Now both killers were level with each other. Neither dare cringe at the other's close proximity. Such a gesture would have invited attack.

Each animal inhaled the other's pungent scent, identified and stored it away for future reference. Both made another careful step forward as they moved parallel to each other. They kept their eyes rigidly to the front but their ears pointed backwards. Each tail stiff; each leg moved with clockwork precision in absolute slow-time as if they were mechanical soldiers.

Slowly, carefully they moved past each other. Their outward appearance was that of total indifference. Inwardly they boiled and bubbled with tenseness ready for instant and deadly attack.

As tail passed tail they kept up their slow gait. Even though they had passed each other without either yielding there was still the time when treachery might arise. Neither looked back; both animals relied upon their sharp ears.

In those silent seconds in which they accomplished such a difficult manoeuvre without loss of face, each animal acknowledged the other as a great warrior and mighty killer. The law had endowed each with the knowledge of what to do should such a tricky situation arise. They had obeyed the law and both lived which was what the law intended. At other times and under different circumstances, like taking meat in a period of shortage, it was quite permissible to fight to the death but the law would not tolerate unnecessary killing between species who rarely overbred. They had to learn to live with each other; to respect each other and, by obeying the inherited rules, there was thus room for both in the wild.

The tree knew it had been a near thing. The prince came out to the space under the great boughs, halted then slowly – almost thoughtfully – retreated to his bed.

The weasel vanished in the undergrowth of the copse. At the entrance to her burrow she too stopped, listened, paused and very slowly walked from sight.

The wind rose and the tree rustled its branches together in sheer relief. It was the most pregnant situation it had witnessed for many a year.

As the dawn strengthened a feeble sun started to disperse the mist and outline the countryside in an insipid winter yellow. There was little real colour because there were few to be attracted by it. Only the sparse red berries dabbed in the hedge broke the monotony of grey, brown and black.

The grass had paled. The dead stems were fawn and brown. The earth was dark red and black from constant damp. The wet also encouraged the moss to grow on the tree's north side which, in turn, provided a snug home for larvae to sleep out the cold months. The moss also kept that side of the tree warm and the law had ensured it gave a further use to spring birds who required a soft bedding material in their nests.

After the one, sharp warning frost the weather changed again to slashing and constant rain which even hinted at sleet. During the times when the rain ceased, mist clung around the hedge corner and curtained the smaller branches and twigs with beads of clammy moisture.

It was silent. Those who stayed active during the winter moved quietly. Danger could be around every bush and clump of grass. Peril in the shape of a hungry belly. The only occasional outbursts of noise came from the birds.

Of all, it was the robin whose voice was loudest as if defying the cold to do its worst. The blackbird would, at times, add her melodious voice and sometimes they would be joined by a flock of starlings as they paused for rest between travelling the countryside and following the food supplies of berries and worms.

The prince was a quiet animal. His trade was stealth. His passage difficult to note and often even the tree was surprised when its friend appeared as if from nowhere. The tree studied its friend anxiously. It could see that the restless feeling in the prince was building up again to an explosive point where anything could happen.

Then one night it did happen. It was cold, clear and the moon shone down and bathed everything in silver. At midnight, when all was eerily still, a sound knifed the air. In the silence the noise carried for a great distance and the tree was glad. It was the sound for which it had been waiting. Now – there would be action. It was a raucous, murderous sound even though muted by distance. To the prince it was the sweetest music he had ever heard.

He stood frozen near the tree. He faced the sound and quivered with excitement. Every nerve twanged with pleasure and the great restlessness and indecision vanished. Now he knew what he wanted. Now – he knew what to do and, more important, where to go.

The vixen screamed her invitation through the night air again. Every fox within miles listened carefully, noted the direction and forgot all other matters.

Out there, way over there a desirable, lovely vixen was telling the world she was lonely. She wanted company. She was interested in being wooed. Would anyone like to come and introduce himself?

The weird shriek knifed the air once more and the prince went. There was no hesitation now. He forgot that he was hungry and had been about to go hunting. His belly could wait – a charming vixen could not. He pushed through the hedge into the field, broke into a lope and, with brush held high, sped across the field. His course unswervingly straight and true as if a radar signal was homing him to the correct bearing.

The tree watched its friend blend into the night and wondered how many other dog foxes were already on the same mission. It mattered not. The prince came from an aristocratic line of powerful fighters and great lovers. It would go hard on any dog fox who thought to steal the prince's vixen if they suited each other.

The tree scanned the horizon with its top branches. Now and again it caught a glimpse of the fox moving at speed then there was the second when its friend was outlined on the crest of a hill. A pause while the animal caught his breath then he descended and was lost to sight.

The tree was glad its friend had followed his destiny at last. Once again it was just the mighty chestnut tree standing solid and foursquare to the wind; defying all the elements, braving the storms and blizzards. But there. Always there. Ready and waiting for all its friends to come back again. The prince would return, of that it was sure and he would not return alone. Until then the tree must wait, watch and stand guard over the cherished little corner which so much of the wildlife called – home.

The publishers hope that this book has given you enjoyable reading. Large Print Books are especially designed to be as easy to see and hold as possible. If you wish a complete list of our books please ask at your local library or write directly to:

Dales Large Print Books
Magna House, Long Preston,
Skipton, North Yorkshire.
BD23 4ND

This Large Print Book, for people
who cannot read normal print,
is published under the auspices of

THE ULVERSCROFT FOUNDATION

APL		CCS	
Cen		Ear	
Mob		Cou	
ALL		Jub	
WH		CHE	
Ald		Bel	
Fin		Fol	
Can		STO	
Til		HCL	